Dorothy Davies

MAMBA'S DAUGHTERS

Plays
by Dorothy and DuBose Heyward

PORGY

MAMBA'S DAUGHTERS

by Dorothy Heyward

NANCY ANN

by DuBose Heyward

BRASS ANKLE

MAMBA'S DAUGHTERS

A PLAY

---

by Dorothy and DuBose Heyward

Dramatized from the novel
MAMBA'S DAUGHTERS
by DuBose Heyward

ILLUSTRATED

FARRAR & RINEHART
INCORPORATED
NEW YORK   TORONTO

CAST OF CHARACTERS

(In the order of their appearance)

MAMBA, *Hagar's mother*
GARDENIA
CHARLESTON NEGROES:
    ANDY
    TESSIE
    JANE
    And others
CLERK OF THE COURT ⎫
BAILIFF ⎪
FIRST POLICEMAN ⎪
SECOND POLICEMAN ⎬ *White*
THE PROSECUTING ATTORNEY ⎪
THE JUDGE ⎪
ST. JULIAN DE CHATINY WENTWORTH (SAINT) ⎭
HAGAR
DAVEY, *Saint's assistant*
NEGROES OF EDIWANDER ISLAND:
    MINGO
    DRAYTON
    EVA
    WILLIE MAY
    NED
    And others
MAUM VINA, *the Island matriarch*
THE REVEREND QUINTUS WHALEY
GILLY BLUTON
DOLLY, *Ned's wife*
LISSA, *as a child*
MARTHA
SLIM
TONY
LISSA, *Hagar's daughter*

The following is a copy of the program of the first performance of "Mamba's Daughters," as presented at the Empire Theater, New York City, Tuesday night, January 3, 1939:

Guthrie McClintic

presents

Ethel Waters

in

MAMBA'S DAUGHTERS

A Play

by

Dorothy and DuBose Heyward

Dramatized from the novel

Mamba's Daughters

by

DuBose Heyward

Characters

(In order of their appearance)

Mamba (Hagar's mother)	*Georgette Harvey*
Gardenia	*Anne Brown*
Andy	*Jimmy Wright*
Jane	*Laura Vaughns*
Tessie	*Dorothy Paul*
Slim	*Reginald Beane*
Policeman	*Barry Kelley*
Another Policeman	*John Rustad*
Clerk of the Court	*John Cornell*
The Prosecuting Attorney	*Oliver Barbour*
St. Julian de Chatiny Wentworth (Saint)	*José Ferrer*
The Judge	*Harry Mestayer*
Hagar	*Ethel Waters*
Davey (Saint's assistant)	*Al Stokes*

NED .... *Hayes Pryor*
MINGO .... *Louis Sharp*
DRAYTON .... *Canada Lee*
MAUM VINA (The Island Matriarch) .... *Ethel Purnello*
EVA .... *Georgia Burke*
WILLIE MAY .... *Helen Dowdy*
THE REVEREND QUINTUS WHALEY .... *J. Rosamond Johnson*
GILLY BLUTON .... *Willie Bryant*
DOLLY (Ned's wife) .... *Alberta Hunter*
LISSA (as a child) .... *Joyce Miller*
MARTHA (Eva's daughter) .... *Rena Mitchell*
LISSA (Hagar's daughter) .... *Fredi Washington*

CHARLESTON COURTROOM VISITORS AND EDIWANDER ISLAND FIELD
HANDS, CHURCH MEMBERS.. *Henry May, Arthur McLean, Rebecca
Champion, Loula Mae McDaniel, Ella
Mae Lashley, Edna Waters, Mary
Holmes, Edna Beane, Fredi Marshall,
Assotta Marshall, Robert Rains, Laura
Vaughns, Dorothy Goosby*

SCENE SYNOPSIS

ACT FOUR

SCENE 1: The Commissary.   Night, the present time.
   (It is the same hour and night as Prologue.)
SCENE 2: Gilly's Cabin.   Later, same night.
SCENE 3: The Commissary.   Later, same night.

The play is complete without the Prologue.   In the opinion of the authors its inclusion heightens the drama of the scenes that follow.

Grateful acknowledgment is made to George W. Hibbitt, Walter C. Garwick, and The Society for the Preservation of Spirituals, of Charleston, for assistance in connection with the spirituals used in this play.

Stage Manager......................*James Neilson*
Stage Manager......................*John Cornell*

Staged by Guthrie McClintic
Settings by Perry Watkins
Special song composed by
Jerome Kern
from lyric by
DuBose Heyward

MAMBA'S ROOM

Stage Setting for Prologue
and Act Two, Scene 3

THE COMMISSARY OF BRICK HOUSE PLANTATION
ON EDIWANDER ISLAND

Stage Setting for Act Two, Scene 1, Act Three, Scene 1,
Act Four, Scenes 1 and 3

COUNTRY CHURCH

Stage Setting for Act Two, Scene 2
(The same setting, with variations, is used for Act Three,
Scene 2, and Act Four, Scene 2)

PROLOGUE

PROLOGUE

TIME: *The present.*

SCENE: MAMBA'S *room in a tenement on the Charleston water front. The entrance door is in back wall, right of center. Door to bedroom in left wall. A window in right wall. The room is an incongruous mixture of poverty and wealth. Most of the furnishings are left-overs from* MAMBA'S *long years of poverty, but there are also the acquisitions of her recent wealth. Her big armchair is expensive-looking and comfortable. Against the left wall near the front stands a large cabinet radio.* MAMBA *sits in the armchair at right, facing the radio. She is a wiry, little old woman with a keen, shrewd face. She wears a neat, black dress. A group of negroes, mostly young, sit on the floor in front of* MAMBA. *They form a half circle, facing radio. Their clothes are like the room: some of them are dressed up and some in work clothes.* GARDENIA *sits at* MAMBA'S *knees. She is one of the well-dressed ones; a mulatto in her late twenties, large, flamboyant, good-natured.* ANDY, *a young man in overalls, is turning the radio dial.*

GARDENIA

What are you galloping all over the dial for? It's coming right over the Charleston station.

ANDY

Yeah, I know, but it won't begin for 'nother three minutes. I jus' seein' what's on the air.

3

MAMBA

Turn um to Cha'ston, den lef' um dere.   I ain't want to miss de beginning an' might be dey ain't know up in Noo Yo'k dat it's still t'ree minute' of nine in Cha'ston.

ANDY

Ain't yo' know, Maum' Mamba, dat when de radio say it nine o'clock it nine o'clock wherever yo' is—Charleston or Noo Yo'k?

GARDENIA

Do like Mamba says. It's her radio, ain't it?   And her broadcast.   You're making her nervous.
[ANDY *turns dial and radio blares loudly.*]
And don't miss the bargains on the first floor—

EVERYBODY

Turn um down.
[ANDY *turns dial.*]

GARDENIA

Down some more, just so we can hear when the chimes ring.

JANE

Is it true, Maum' Mamba, dat dey pays Lissa a t'ousand dollah jes' fo' dis one broadcast?

MAMBA

[*Vehemently.*]
No, it ain't true.   Dat big talk an' I wish folks would stop talkin' dat way.   'Tain't likely dey would pay my grand-

daughter all dat money when she's jus' beginning, is it? De day comin' mebbe when dey goin' pay my Lissa as much money as any singer in de worl' but dis de firs' time she sing on a big broadcas' like dis'.

TESSIE

[Very importantly.]

You know, Maum' Mamba, when I was in Noo Yo'k and went with your grand-daughter to dat re-hearsal, dey got dat big chorus dat sings with her and she—

MAMBA

[Impatiently.]

Yo' done tole me dat.

[Apparently all the negroes are fed up with accounts of TESSIE's *trip to New York.]*

TESSIE

Yes, but I ain't told you how Lissa—

GARDENIA

Tell her later. Can't you see she's got her mind on other things?

JANE

Hagar ain't going to get here now.

GARDENIA

[Comfortingly to MAMBA.*]*

Maybe she'll come yet. Don't you worry, Mamba.

ANDY

[*His ear to radio.*]
Dis radio's got de damnedest way of fadin' out on yo'.

MAMBA

[*Very sarcastic.*]
I suppose dat little radio you got upstairs is a lot better dan dis one.

TESSIE

Yo' know, Maum' Mamba, you musn't expect to hear Lissa sing when de concert firs' begin.   At dat rehearsal Lissa took me to, firs' de chorus sang, den a man an' den—

GARDENIA

Ain't it time yet, Andy?

ANDY

No. It's still the Charleston local.

JANE

Mebbe Hagar got mixed up on the day.   You shore she know tonight was the night?

MAMBA

Don' ask foolish question', gal.   Dat gal of mine has been countin' de days for weeks.

ANDY

[*His ear to radio.*]
Shut up, everybody.   Charleston's signing off.
    [*Turns up radio.*]

RADIO.—*Announcer:* Station WWSC atop the Francis Marion Hotel down in Charleston, South Carolina. *Chimes.* Nine o'clock, Randall's Soup time. When you think of soup, think of Randall's. We now rejoin the National network. *An orchestra plays with vim a few bars of a triumphant march. Second Announcer, impressively:* "The Sultana Hour!"

ANDY

Dat ain't it, is it?

TESSIE

Shore dat is.

GARDENIA

Keep quiet.

RADIO.—*Orchestra plays in low key. Announcer, talking through music,* The makers of Sultana Cigarettes have the honor to present the initial broadcast of their new coast-to-coast program, AMERICA SINGS. *A low hum of a large chorus begins. Announcer:* In our program tonight we celebrate the negroes' greatest gift to America—the gift of song, featuring the lovely voice of the new colored singer—LISSA WENTWORTH. We are bringing you tonight, in honor of our star, the songs of her home land—the low country of South Carolina. Our first number is a spiritual sung for you by the chorus, "Don' Ya Mind What De Debil Do." *As he finishes speaking the humming grows louder.*

Baritone: Don' ya mind what de debil do.
Chorus: Don' ya mind.
Baritone: Don' ya mind what de debil do.
Chorus: Don' ya mind, oh, don' ya mind what de
    debil do,
    He can't get to heaben an' he won't let you,
    Don' ya mind.
Chorus hums between verses.

JANE

[*Talking through humming.*]
I does wonder what could be keeping Hagar.

TESSIE

It seems mighty funny after Lissa sent dis big radio espe-
cial so as her mother an' grandma could hear her sing good
dat her ma ain't even take de trouble to come up from de
Island.

GARDENIA

They've got radios on the Island.   You can just bet Lissa's
mother's listening in somewhere.   [*To* MAMBA.]   Might be
the spring tide's over the causeway and cut the Island off
from Charleston but Hagar's listening to this somewhere.
You know that, Mauma.

MAMBA

[*Slowly, shaking head.*]
I ain't neber know nuttin' 'bout dat daughter of mine less
I got my eye right on her.

TESSIE

Now listen, Mauma Mamba, dis is going to be Lissa.
  RADIO.—*Baritone:* Don' yo mind what de preacher do.

TESSIE

No, dat ain't Lissa.
  [MAMBA *gives her a withering look.*]
  RADIO.—*Chorus:* Don' ya mind, etc.
  [NOTE: *It does not matter whether or not the negroes'
  actual words are distinctly heard above music. Obvi-
  ously, their talking distresses* MAMBA.]

ANDY

Dey ain't sing dat de same as we sing it in Chas'ton.

A MAN

Dem Harlem niggers ain't know how sing spirituals.

JANE

Wish dey'd hurry up an' get to Lissa.

GARDENIA

Can't you all keep quiet?
  RADIO.—*Humming between verses.*
  [*The audience on stage begins gradually swaying to the
  music. Several beat their hands softly to its rhythm.
  Radio fades.*]

EVERYBODY

Turn um up.
  [*Andy turns it up.*]

RADIO.—*Baritone:* Don' ya mind what de deacon do.
Chorus: Don' ya mind.
Baritone: Don' ya mind what de deacon do.
Chorus, augmented by several voices on stage:
     Don' ya mind,
     Oh, don' ya mind what de deacon do.
Chorus and audience: He can't git to heaben
     an' he won't let you,
     Don' ya mind.
The spiritual ends and applause comes over radio.
[*The listeners comment volubly.*]

TESSIE

[*Getting to her feet.*]
Lissen, Maum' Mamba, next a big, fat woman's goin' to
sing. She's got an awful fine voice but she's the fattest thing
you ever—
     RADIO.—*Orchestra begins to play "That Hallelujah
     Song."*
     [*They all recognize it.*]

JANE
Hagar's song.

MAMBA

[*With deep indignation to* TESSIE.]
Yo' ain't tellin' me anybody but Lissa goin' sing dis song.

TESSIE

[*Looking discomfited.*]
I thought—

RADIO.—*Announcer, talking through music:* And now,
LISSA WENTWORTH.

ANDY
Atta baby!

JANE
Yo' ain't know so much, Tessie.

RADIO.—*A lovely soprano voice begins "That Hallelu-
jah Song."*

[*For a minute all the negroes listen in rapt silence. A
far-away look comes into* MAMBA'S *eyes.* TESSIE *still
on her feet begins to sway and to clasp her hands on
her breast as though she fancies she, herself, is singing. The half-circle on floor lay their arms across
each other's and all sway together. Radio plays
loudly.*]

EVERYBODY
Turn um down.

[ANDY *turns it too far.*]

EVERYBODY
Turn um up.

[*Another negro takes dial from* ANDY *and begins to
turn it.*]

NEGRO
I'll see if I can get it over another station.

EVERYBODY
Stop dat. Turn em back. Lef' it be. Turn em to Cha's-
ton.

[*He reluctantly obeys. They all begin to sway again
and then to moan a low accompaniment. ANDY has
difficulty in keeping his feet still; executes a few dance
steps but intercepts a furious look from GARDENIA
and stops.*]

TESSIE
[*Continuing to gesture.*]
Look, Maum' Mamba, like dis.
[*MAMBA looks at her. Seeing that she is getting atten-
tion TESSIE puts on steam.*]

MAMBA
[*Witheringly.*]
Yo' t'ink I needs yo' fo' show me my Lissa. [*Pause.*]
I can see her so plain. If you folks would let me be, I can
see her just lak she's standin' there— [*Trance-like.*] Mebbe
not lak she looks in her grand Noo Yo'k clothes— [*To GAR-
DENIA.*] I see her singing that firs' song in church. [*To
negroes.*] Yo' all let me be so's I can see her.
[*GARDENIA gets up and takes ANDY by arm, propels
him toward door, opens it.*]

GARDENIA
Go on up and turn on your own radio. [*Gestures imperi-
ously toward the others. Reluctantly they obey.*] Sh—go
along, we're all bothering Mamba. You can listen in on
Andy's radio.
[*Obediently but slowly they go out the door. MAMBA
is gazing fixedly at radio; she seems unconscious of*

their movements. A few rebels require hard looks from GARDENIA *but at last they are all gone.* GARDENIA *comes back to* MAMBA, *stands back of her chair, her hand on* MAMBA'S *shoulder.*]

MAMBA

I can see um singin' dis one, Gardenia, when she wan't more'n five year old.

RADIO.—LISSA *concludes song. Applause.*

MAMBA

Yo' go, too, Gardenia. I can see um better by myself.

RADIO.—LISSA *speaks:* Thank you. I am so happy that you like that song because it is a song my mother used to sing when I was a child. And the song I am going to sing for you next is also a song I learned from my mother. I am so happy tonight that I hope you will forgive me if I am very sentimental. I know that somewhere way down South my mother is listening to me and on this—the biggest night of my life—I want her to hear me say, "Mother, I owe this all—to you." *Some applause.*

GARDENIA

Gosh! Won't that set Hagar up!

MAMBA

Mebbe she ain't hear it.

GARDENIA

You can bet your last dollar she did. Stop worrying, Mamba, and enjoy your big night.

MAMBA

[*Never moving her eyes from the radio but reaching up
a hand to pat the hand on her shoulder. Slowly.*]
I ain't neber easy in my mind when I don' know what dat
daughter of mine is up to.

RADIO.—*The orchestra begins to play "Lonesome
Walls."*

[GARDENIA *bends down and kisses* MAMBA'S *forehead
and softly goes out the door, closes it behind her.*]

RADIO.—*Announcer, through the music:* It is from a
race's suffering rather than from its joy that its most
poignant folk music springs. From the jails and
penitentiaries in the Deep South comes this haunting
song, "Lonesome Walls." Ready, Miss Wentworth. LISSA *sings "Lonesome Walls."*

[*Halfway through the first verse the light begins to
fade. It lingers on* MAMBA, *who holds her arms as
though she sheltered a baby. She sways from the
waist gently, to and fro. The radio dial goes dark.
Then the stage is in complete darkness while* LISSA
*sings on. After she has finished the song the orchestra
plays until it is cut short by the voice of the bailiff
calling for Order in the Court.*]

ACT ONE

ACT ONE

TIME: *Twenty years ago.*

SCENE: *In the semi-darkness the* BAILIFF's *voice is heard calling for order in the court.*

The lights come on revealing a small courtroom. The JUDGE's *desk is at left center,* CLERK's *desk at left front. The entrance door is in right wall, door by which prisoners enter in back wall at left. Door to* JUDGE's *private office is in left wall at front. The prisoners' dock is at back, witness chair at left.*

There are six rows of seats. The last two rows are packed with negroes. There are several negroes in fourth row with MAMBA *in aisle seat (identical spot on stage which she occupied at end of prologue). She is holding a young baby.*

SAINT JULIAN WENTWORTH (SAINT) *sits alone in second row.*

Policemen stand at the doors. The PROSECUTING ATTORNEY, *whose official title in South Carolina is "The Solicitor," sits waiting near left front.*

CLERK

His Honor, the Judge. Everybody rise.

[*Everybody stands.* JUDGE *enters and sits at desk. He is a kindly, middle-aged gentleman, somewhat negligent in his dress. His robe, because of the hot weather, is pushed as far back as possible and trails like a cape*

17

behind him. Everybody resumes seats. JUDGE studies papers on desk. SOLICITOR rises and stands waiting. The JUDGE looks up and sees SAINT. Nods to him. Looks questioningly at him. SAINT gets up and goes down to desk. Shakes hands with JUDGE.]

SAINT

Good morning, Cousin Ronald.

JUDGE

Good morning, Saint. What brings you up from Ediwander Plantation in the middle of cabbage season?

SAINT

[Disgustedly.]
Jury duty, as usual.

JUDGE

Good man and true, eh! *[SAINT smiles and nods. JUDGE turning his attention to papers on desk.]* Well, look me up during the first recess and tell me all the Wentworth news.

SAINT

There's never any news in the Wentworth family but I will look you up.

[He returns to his seat. MAMBA overhears the conversation and half rises to look at SAINT. The JUDGE confers briefly with PROSECUTING ATTORNEY.]

JUDGE
Call the first case.

CLERK
  Hagar.

FIRST POLICEMAN
  Hagar.

SECOND POLICEMAN
  Hagar.

  [HAGAR *is led in, stands at dock. She is a young woman
  of large proportions, unusually tall, unusually broad
  and giving an immediate impression of great strength.
  Above her superb body is a pleasant, childlike face.
  She now looks frightened and bewildered, yet there
  is dignity about her. From her entrance she keeps
  her eyes riveted on the* JUDGE'S *face as though she
  hoped to read his meaning there rather than in his
  puzzling words.*]

JUDGE
  Is the prisoner represented by counsel?

PROSECUTING ATTORNEY
  No, your honor.

JUDGE
                    [*To* HAGAR.]
  What's your name?

HAGAR
  Hagar, yo' honoh.

JUDGE
  What's your last name?

HAGAR
Jes' Hagar, Boss.

JUDGE
Your *last* name, I say.
[HAGAR *stares, mystified.*]

HAGAR
Hagar.

PROSECUTING ATTORNEY
That's right, your honor—Hagar.   We've had her up here half a dozen times and it's always just Hagar.   If she's got any more name, she doesn't know what it is.   That old woman's her mother.   [*To* MAMBA.]   Hey, you, Auntie! This is your daughter, isn't she?

MAMBA
[*Rising and curtsying.*]
Yes, boss, yo' honoh.   De Lor' hab mercy, but dat my daughter.

JUDGE
Is your daughter's name the same as yours?

MAMBA
Oh, no!   Yo' honoh!   She Hagar, I Mamba.

JUDGE
Mamba what?

MAMBA

Mamba.   Dat's all, yo' honoh.

JUDGE

You've got a last name, haven't you?

MAMBA

Fo' shore I gots las' name, yo' honoh.

JUDGE

Well, what is it?

> [MAMBA *looks around wildly and her eye lights on* SAINT.]

MAMBA

Oh, now I 'members.   My las' name Wentwut, yo' honoh.

JUDGE

Wentwut?

MAMBA

Wentwut. Dat right—same as dat genl'man dere.

> [*She indicates* SAINT.]

JUDGE

> [*Smiling at* SAINT.]

Well, you have selected a distinguished family.

> [SAINT *answers* JUDGE's *smile with a helpless gesture.*]

JUDGE

> [*Studying papers.*]

Hagar, I see that you are charged with assault and battery

with intent to kill. Also with indecent exposure of your person. Do you plead guilty or not guilty?

HAGAR

I'se guilty, yo' honoh.

JUDGE

The Solicitor has detailed the facts connected with this case to which you have entered the plea of guilty. But in order to satisfy my own mind, I will ask you a few questions before passing sentence. Did you or did you not beat this man?

HAGAR

Yes, yo' honoh, I fit um.

JUDGE

Did you intend to kill him?

HAGAR

No, yo' honoh. I ain't even mean to hurt um—not *much*.

JUDGE

Why did you attack him. [*Pause.*] Why did you fight him?

HAGAR

He won't pay fo' he clothes.

JUDGE

Did you sell him some clothes?

HAGAR

No, Jedge, I ain't sell um none. I wash um.

JUDGE

I see.   He refused to pay for his wash?

HAGAR

Yes, Jedge.

JUDGE

You were intoxicated at the time?   [*Pause.*]   You were drunk?

HAGAR

Yes, suh, he done drunk me.

JUDGE

Oh, you had been drinking with him?

HAGAR

Yes, suh.

JUDGE

Then, there is a charge of indecent exposure.   Why did you remove your clothing?   [*Pause.*]   Why did you take off your clothes?

HAGAR

I ain't take um off, yo' honoh.   He take um off.

JUDGE

While you were drinking with him?

HAGAR

No, yo' honoh.   While I fit um.

JUDGE

Why didn't you stop him?

HAGAR

I ain't could stop um 'cause I ain't got de use ob my han's.

JUDGE

You didn't have the use of your hands?

HAGAR

No, yo' honoh.

JUDGE

Why didn't you have the use of your hands?

HAGAR

Count of dere bein' 'roun' his neck.

JUDGE

Then you *were* trying to strangle him?

HAGAR

No, suh, I ain't want to strangle um daid, jes' enough to persuade him to pay fo' he wash.

JUDGE

Then how do you account for the fact that at the hospital they thought for a time he might not live?

HAGAR

I guess I ain't know how hard I hold um count of me bein' drunk.

JUDGE

Are there any extenuating circumstances you would like to tell me?   [*Pause.*]   Have you told me everything that happened?

HAGAR

[*Considers.*]

Yes, yo' honoh.

JUDGE

[*Sternly.*]

The prisoner will stand up.   [HAGAR *rises.*]   The charge against you in this case is assault and battery with intent to kill.   Had the man been killed the charge would have been murder and the penalty death.   But the man escaped with his life, therefore the charge is one of lesser degree—the records show, moreover, that you have been repeatedly arrested on charges of disorderly conduct while under the influence of liquor and that you have served two sentences in jail for minor offences. [*He pauses portentously.*] I, therefore, sentence you to five years' penal servitude in the state penitentiary.

> [MAMBA *moans.   The sympathetic audience in last two rows loudly echo her moan.   The* POLICEMAN *shouts, "Order in the court."* JUDGE *studies papers on desk. Beckons to* PROSECUTING ATTORNEY, *who brings papers and discusses them with the* JUDGE.   *The* CLERK *joins them.   Their conference which is inaudible to the audience consumes five minutes and during it the court room relaxes.   Jurors move about.*

Occupants of the benches come and go. POLICEMAN
goes to lead HAGAR *out. She looks toward* MAMBA.
*Holds out arms—not fully outstretched, only a timid
gesture of longing. Without a word,* MAMBA *rises
and comes down aisle, carrying baby.* POLICEMAN
does not interfere. MAMBA *lifts the baby toward
her.* HAGAR *takes it in her arms. She does not kiss
it nor clutch it to her. She only holds it, looking
down at it with infinite sadness and longing. After
a moment* POLICEMAN *touches her on shoulder. Instantly obedient, she slowly stretches baby toward*
MAMBA, *who takes it. She looks appealingly into*
MAMBA's *eyes, silently entreating her.*]

MAMBA

Dat all right, daughtuh.   Yo' ma ain't let no harm come
to Lissa.

[HAGAR *is led out.* MAMBA *stands looking after her.
She continues to stand there as though not knowing
what to do next until she sees* POLICEMAN *motioning
with his head that she can't stand there. Then suddenly resolute, she goes to* POLICEMAN *at entrance
door.*]

MAMBA

Mr. Officer, 'scuse me.   Who dat gen'lman settin' dere?

POLICEMAN

What gentleman?

MAMBA

De one de jedge call Mr. Wentwut.

POLICEMAN

Oh, that's St. Julian de Chatiny Wentworth, if you want it all.

MAMBA

Him frien' of de jedge, ain't it?

POLICEMAN

He's a cousin or something, I believe.

MAMBA

He got pull wid de jedge, mebbe. [*The* POLICEMAN *brushes her impatiently away.*] T'ank yo' kindly, Mr. Cap'n.
[SAINT *gets up and walks down aisle toward door. Saint Julian Wentworth is the type of Southern gentleman that the city of Charleston is convinced no other community can grow. His face is high bred, sensitive. His voice low and pleasant. His accent Southern but not exaggerated. His manner is courteous to both whites and blacks. He is about thirty and is now dressed in his city clothes, which are worn but well cut and well pressed.* MAMBA *blocks his way.*]

MAMBA

[*Curtsying low.*]

How yo' is, Mr. Saint?

SAINT

Who told you you could take the name of Wentworth?

MAMBA

T'ink of yo' axin' dat! But den I guess yo' was too little fo' 'member. But I been keepin' my eye on yo' all dese yeahs, askin' eberybody how Mr. Saint gettin' 'long.

SAINT

Are you trying to tell me that your name really is Wentworth?

MAMBA

Shore it is, Mr. Saint. Wentworth since the day my grandpappy belong to yo' grandpa down on de ole Ediwander plantation. And when de wah come—

SAINT

What's the game, Mamba?

MAMBA

De what, Mr. Saint?

SAINT

What do you want of me?   Money?

MAMBA

[*Really hurt.*]
No, Mr. Saint.   I swear to Gawd I ain't want money.

SAINT

What *do* you want?

MAMBA

[*Made bold by her love.*]
Mr. Saint, dis chile in bery great trouble.

SAINT

Nonsense. You've had hard luck, I admit. But that baby's not worrying about it.
[*Turns to go. MAMBA follows.*]

MAMBA

Mr. Saint, what I goin' do wid dis chile?

SAINT

How should I know? It's your daughter's child?

MAMBA

Yes, suh.

SAINT

Well, you're its grandmother. You can look after it, can't you?

MAMBA

What I goin' feed it?

SAINT

Well, it looks very young. I should advise you to feed it milk.

MAMBA
Milk?

SAINT
[*Slightly annoyed.*]
You've heard of milk, I suppose?

MAMBA
[*Desperately.*]
But dey sendin' it ma away.

SAINT
[*Embarrassed.*]
Oh—er—I see.   It's a nursing baby?   Well—er—I really
don't see that there's anything I can do about that.

MAMBA
Dat bery dangerous fo' mek change so sudden wid de hot
wedder comin' on.

SAINT
Well, from what I heard this morning, your daughter
can't be a very good mother to the child.

MAMBA
My gal?

SAINT
Yes.

MAMBA

Mr. Saint, dis chile my daughter's life. Mine, too.

SAINT

[Thoughtfully.]

Well—I might speak about it to the judge for you. I don't know what they do in such cases.

[Again turns to go.]

MAMBA

[Following him.]

T'ank yo' so bery kindly, Mr. Saint. Yo' bery kin'. Dis gal chile goin' to be brought up prayin' de Lor' to bless yo'. Yo' see what a purty baby she is?

SAINT

[Bored, but kindly.]

Yes, a fine baby.

[Again starts down aisle.]

MAMBA

[Following.]

An' one t'ing more, Mr. Saint *[very earnestly]*, not fo' me but fo' my daughtuh an' my daughtuh's daughtuh. Dese two female born fo' trouble. *[SAINT reluctantly turns back to her. Mysteriously.]* Dere's t'ings about dis case de jedge don't know nuttin' 'bout.

SAINT

Why didn't your daughter tell him when she had the chance?

MAMBA

Dat gal—she ain't got good sense by sheself. It take the two of we fo' she to talk. [SAINT *looks hesitant.* MAMBA *is quick to follow up her advantage.*] My gal ain't had no white folks to speak up fo' she so de jedge ain't take de trouble fo' find out. Mr. Saint, it wouldn't cos' yo' nuttin' to speak one little word fo' my gal.

[SAINT *goes down aisle to desk. Speaks in low tone to* JUDGE, *who as he listens, looks speculatively down aisle at* MAMBA.]

JUDGE

What has she been telling you?

SAINT

She's been telling me the facts of life. Do you know where little babies get their dinners? It seems they get them out of their mothers.

JUDGE

You didn't know that, Saint? Why, I've known that for years. [*Seriously.*] Do you feel that there's an adequate reason for reopening the case?

SAINT

Cousin Ronald, I think I know negroes. Down on the island I scarcely see a white face from one week-end to the next. I believe that there's more to it than you heard.

JUDGE
[*To* POLICEMAN.]
Where is the woman Hagar?

POLICEMAN
She's outside waiting for the wagon.

JUDGE
Have her brought back. [*To* SAINT *while they wait, meditatively.*] So it's a nursing baby? I didn't think of that. Poor devils, why do they always have to get themselves into so much trouble? [HAGAR *is led in. Takes place in dock.* SAINT *resumes seat.*] Hagar, Mr. Wentworth has persuaded me to reconsider your case.

HAGAR
[*Suddenly all smiles.*]
I t'ank yo' kindly, yo' honoh. I t'ank yo' kindly, suh.

JUDGE
Mr. Solicitor.
[HAGAR's *smiles quickly vanish. She is again frightened.*]

PROSECUTING ATTORNEY
Hagar, the judge thinks that perhaps he has not heard your whole story. Will you tell him in your own words exactly what happened?

HAGAR

[*Looks down a minute.   Then up at* JUDGE.]

I gone to the wharf to take um he clothes.   An' he won't pay me.   So I fit um.

SAINT

Your honor, I suggest that you let the old woman take the stand.   She's bright and the daughter is apparently—er—inarticulate.

JUDGE

Just a minute.   Hagar, think hard and try to tell us everything that happened, from the time you reached the boat until the police came.   [HAGAR *thinks hard but to no effect.*] What did you say to the man when you took him his wash?

HAGAR

I say, "Here yo' wash.   It two dollah."

JUDGE

And what did he say?

HAGAR

He say, "Fotch um aboard, sistuh."   So I fotch um aboard fo' um, 'cause it was a big, heavy box an' he was a puny little man.   I take um down in de engine room.

JUDGE

What then?

HAGAR

I say, "Look um over an' if he like you like um, dat's two dollah. If anyt'ing ain't like you like um, I do um over."

JUDGE

And then?

HAGAR

He say, "What's yo' hurry, sistuh? Set down an' rest a spell."

JUDGE

Yes?

HAGAR

An' I say, "It shore is hot." An' I set down. [*Seems to come to a full stop. Looks questioningly at* JUDGE. *Sees he wants more.*] Den he say, "Hab a little drink." An' I say, "No, I t'ank yo' kindly." An' he say, "Jus' a little one." An' I say, "I t'ank yo' kindly but I don't drink no more now I got a baby, 'case my ma say licker ain't good fo' um." An' he say, "Well, set an' res'." So I sets an' rests.

[*Comes to a full stop. Looks at* JUDGE *with her great questioning eyes.*]

MAMBA

He know dat gal is weak an' he advantage he'self on her weakness.

PROSECUTING ATTORNEY
Did you say weak?

MAMBA
He know she like licker an' he know she like to sing.
[*To* HAGAR.]   Tell um, daughtuh.

HAGAR
Then he take up he guitar an' begin fo' strum um.   An'
pretty soon he begin fo' sing.

MAMBA
[*Unable to restrain herself.*]
He do dat a purpose—de ole debil—'cause he know 'bout
my daughtuh.   Eberybody know 'bout my daughtuh.   Yo'
honoh, seems lak nuttin' can hold dat daughtuh ob mine from
singin'.   Dat gal was born singin'.

JUDGE
Sit down, old woman, and keep quiet.   You must not in-
terrupt unless you're asked.   [*To* HAGAR.]   He got to singing and then you got to singing?   Is that it?

HAGAR
Firs', I get to pattin' my foot an' den I get to clappin' my
han' an' den he say, "Hab a little drink, sistuh."   An' I say,
"Well, jus' a little one."   An' den I get to singin'.

JUDGE
And then?

HAGAR

> [*After a moment's thought.*]

Eberybody get to singin'.

JUDGE

Everybody? There was more people on the boat?

HAGAR

No, yo' honoh. Jes' him an' me. But I guess after a while de two odder men he got on de boat dey come aboard but de nigger dat was singin' was mos'ly on de wharf. Dey gather 'roun'.

MAMBA

> [*Proudly.*]

When Hagar sing dey allus gather 'roun'.

HAGAR

An' purty soon dat little boat fair rock wid de pure song.

JUDGE

Go on.

HAGAR

Dat go on quite a while an' he keep fillin' up my cup an' I ain't pay attention to um count of we was all singin'. Mebbe I drink quite a bit an' maybe it jus' 'cause I ain't drink anyt'ing at all since I gets my baby, but I a little drunk wid de licker an' I very drunk wid de singin'.

JUDGE

Go on.

HAGAR

Den all of a sudden de whistle blow an' de man git up an' start de engine. An' he hois' me up an' push me up de ladder an' out on de wharf. An' I holler, "Gimme my two dollah." An' he jus' stan' dere grinnin'. Den I see de boat was movin', so I reaches over de side an' I take um roun' de neck an' I lif' um out of de boat up onto de wharf. An' den I shake um an' he grab de front of my dress an' tear um off me. Tear my underbody, too, den all de people on de wharf see I's nekked an' dey laughs an' dat mek me mad. So I shake um some more.

JUDGE
  Yes?

HAGAR

[Thinks.]
  Dat's all. De police come den an' take um to de hospital.
    [Looks questioningly at JUDGE. *The* JUDGE *looks down at his desk as though having some difficulty in controlling his features.]*

JUDGE
  Hagar, I must admit that you seem to have had some provocation. Have you anything to suggest, Mr. Solicitor?

PROSECUTING ATTORNEY
  It seems to me that the trouble with this woman is that she is too simple-minded—er—I don't mean just that—too defenseless—

JUDGE

You don't mean just *that*, do you, Mr. Solicitor?

PROSECUTING ATTORNEY

I mean that she is not—er—equipped by nature to cope with city life. I believe that if she'd been a country negro there wouldn't have been a steadier or more hard-working negro in the district. Would you consider suspending that penitentiary sentence and sending her out of town?

JUDGE

I think you have hit upon the solution. [*To* HAGAR.] Have you any relatives living in the country?

HAGAR

No, suh, yo' honoh. Dere's jus' me an' my ma an' my baby an' we lib in Charleston.

MAMBA

[*Jumping to her feet.*]
Here's Mr. Wentwut. He lib in de country.

JUDGE

[*Grinning maliciously at* SAINT.]
A splendid idea.

SAINT

I beg your pardon, your honor. My residence is here in town. I don't live on Ediwander Island. I only manage the commissary there.

JUDGE

You spend every day there, don't you?

SAINT

Yes, but—

JUDGE

That will be sufficient. And also quite appropriate. [*To* HAGAR.] The prisoner will stand up! [HAGAR *is again frightened but manages to rise.*] Since passing sentence upon you, facts and circumstances have come to my attention of which I was not aware at that time. And as I have authority under the law to change or modify that sentence at any time before you commence to serve it, I have now recalled you for that purpose. I release you upon the condition that you go to the plantation of Mr. St. Julian de Chatiny Wentworth, who has magnanimously agreed to observe your conduct and make regular reports on same to this court. It is an express condition of this release, however, that during the period of five years, you do not return, under any circumstances, to the city of Charleston. If you violate this condition and return, you will have to serve the full term of five years in the penitentiary. Am I clearly understood?

HAGAR

Yes, suh, yo' honoh. T'ank yo', suh. I un'erstan' dat.

JUDGE

Very well. You're free to go with Mr. Wentworth now. [HAGAR *steps down. Goes down aisle to* MAMBA.

Takes the baby from her. The JUDGE *is in confer-
ence with* PROSECUTING ATTORNEY. CLERK *lays
papers before him.* JUDGE *gives directions to* POLICE-
MAN, *who goes out. In other words, the* JUDGE *keeps
busy while:*]

MAMBA

Mr. Saint, I t'ank yo' kindly. May de good Gawd bless
an' keep yo'. Yo' got work fo' my gal on dat plantation?

SAINT

If your daughter were a man, I'd gladly get her a job
but—

MAMBA

[*Proudly.*]

Dere ain't no work a man can do what my daughtuh,
Hagar, can't do.

SAINT

Evidently not. Well, I'll get her on as a field hand.
You can tell her to wait and I'll drive her down after court
closes. I'll ask the judge to release me from jury duty.
[*He turns toward the* JUDGE.]

MAMBA

Mr. Saint.

SAINT

[*Turning back.*]

Well, what now?

MAMBA

I go, too, an' take care of the baby while Hagar work.

SAINT

Oh, my God! Three of you!

MAMBA

Not for long, Mr. Saint. Only six weeks. Den she'll wean Lissa an' I'll bring her back to give her a town raisin'— Please, Mr. Saint—

SAINT

[*Surrendering.*]
Well, I suppose so.

PROSECUTING ATTORNEY

[*Grinning.*]
The white man's burden, eh!

SAINT

[*Under his breath amiably.*]
Damn you!

JUDGE

Next case.

CLERK

[*Rising.*]

Julia Brown.

BAILIFF

Julia Brown.

CURTAIN

ACT TWO

ACT TWO

SCENE 1: *The commissary of Brick House Plantation on Ediwander Island on a May evening, fifteen years ago.*

The counter extends along the wall at right and more than half the length of back wall.

In back wall to left of center a door opens onto a porch. Several windows, one of them back of counter, give onto porch. A second door in left wall leads to SAINT WENT-WORTH'S *room.* SAINT'S *desk stands against this wall. Before it is a swivel chair. There is a tin stove in corner at left back.*

Behind the counter are shelves stocked with country store merchandise. Several dresses, one a flamboyant purple, hang just to the left of entrance door.

During this scene the negroes are going in and out, congregating in groups in the store or on the porch, occasionally talking through the windows to those inside, or going off in their work clothes to return later dressed for church. There are always one or two on the porch till the final scene when all are gone, leaving HAGAR *and* MAMBA *completely alone.*

VINA, *the plantation matriarch, a very old negress, is sitting on a keg at right front, smoking her pipe. This seems to be her special place, as she returns to it from time to time shooing off any other sitter.* SAINT WENTWORTH *and his assistant* DAVEY *are back of the counter.* DAVEY *is serving customers.* SAINT *stands back of cash drawer which is just*

45

under edge of counter near center back. His hair is now gray at the temples, making him look even more distinguished notwithstanding that he is in shirt sleeves.

SAINT

Hurry up. Anybody who wants to buy anything more tonight must make up his mind. I'm going to lock this cash drawer in five minutes.

NED

Don't lock dat drawer, Mr. Saint, till you mek' little change fo' me.

MINGO

Me, too.
[*Several other negroes move up to counter feeling in their pockets.*]

DRAYTON

I wants dis all in dime'. Change um fo' me, will yo', Mr. Saint?

SAINT

[*Making change.*]
Big crap game at Bluton's shack, eh?

DRAYTON

Do, Mr. Saint! We got to hab some change fo' de meetin' tonight.

DAVEY

And after de meetin' dere's a love feast.

SAINT

And after the love feast there's a crap game and by daylight Gilly Bluton will have your shirts. Don't you know
why Gilly *always* wins?

MINGO

Sho' we knows dat, Mr. Saint—de dice is crooked.

DAVEY

But de police neber raids him an' ef yo' plays anywheres
else yo' gits arrested.

MINGO

Den yo' don't eben hab' no fun fo' yo' money.

[*The* REVEREND QUINTUS WHALEY *comes in greeted
by the beaming smiles of all the women. He wears
a black tail coat and alpaca vest across which hangs a
heavy gold watch chain. He is a big man with small
cunning eyes and a large sensuous mouth from which
issues a magnificent sonorous voice. His movements
are ponderous and not without a certain massive dignity. The women crane forward to warm themselves
in the light of his countenance.*]

EVA

Good evenin', Reverend.

WHALEY

Good evenin', good evenin'.

WILLIE MAY

How yo' is, Reverend?

WHALEY

I good, t'ank yo'. How yo' baby, Eva?

EVA

Poorly, t'ank yo', kindly, Reverend.

WHALEY

I'll pray fo' um special at de sarvice tonight. Remember, eberybody, sarvice goin' to begin prompt at seben tonight so's we can finish 'em up early an' start de love feast. Eberybody be prompt.

NEGROES

Yes. We be dere, Reverend. We ain't miss love feast.
[WHALEY *goes to the counter.*]

WHALEY

[*Effusively.*]
Good evenin', Mr. Saint.

SAINT

[*Brusquely.*]
Good evening, Whaley.

WHALEY

Yo' got any more dat good bacon yo' had?

SAINT
> Davey will wait on you in a minute.
>
> [DAVEY *finishes serving* NED, *takes* WHALEY'S *order, which is much larger than any other customer's. It takes* DAVEY *quite a while.* SAINT *comes from behind counter and sits at desk.*]

EVA
> Whar Dolly tonight, Ned?

NED
> Oh, I guess she home whar she belong. I does de fambly buyin'. I ain't believe in women folks forever settin' 'roun' de store when dere chillun need um at home.
>
> [*Starts off with his purchases.*]

WILLIE MAY
> [*Calling after him derisively as he goes out of door.*]
> Ole rooster wid young pullet oughtn't to crow so loud.
> [*Laughter.*]

VINA
> [*Soberly.*]
> You hadn't ought to laugh at ole Ned like dat. Dat can't do no good. What if Gilly Bluton is run after Ned's Dolly, he done de same by plenty odder gal roun' here.

WILLIE MAY
> Well, he ain't got no right to strut so.

VINA
> Lissen, daughtuh, when a man know dat anodder man is runnin' after he 'oman, dat one t'ing. But when he know

dat odder people know, too, den he goin' fight.   Yo' mus'
want to hab killin' on dis plantation, enty?

WILLIE MAY

[*Defiantly.*]

Well, Gilly ain't no Gawd.   He can bleed same as any
odder man.   What de matter wid dose men roun' here,
anyhow, dey 'fraid um so?

[*Casts scornful look around the circle which the men
ignore.*]

DRAYTON

Shut up, gal.   It ain't healthy to get into no trouble wid
Gilly.   He stan's *so*— [*holds up two fingers close together*]
—wid de police.   He can do what he please 'cause he got de
law behin' him.

VINA

[*Undaunted.*]

Willie May didn't use to talk lak dat 'bout Gilly.   Mus'
be he quit goin' to her house now.

[*A few chuckles at this.*]

DRAYTON

[*In doorway.*]

Good evenin', sistuh.   You comin' to de love feast tonight?

HAGAR

[*From porch.*]

I shore am, brudduh.   [HAGAR *comes in.   She smiles*

*greetings to her friends. Pauses by the purple dress to ad-
mire it.*] How much dis dress, Davey?

DAVEY

Persisely same price it was las' week.

WHALEY

[*Reprovingly.*]
You ain't see Davey got a customer, sistuh?

HAGAR

[*Contritely.*]
'Scuse me, Reverend. Guess I fergit my mannahs.
[*A car is heard stopping outside. The negroes on porch
are much interested in it.*]

WILLIE MAY

Hagar time mos' up an' she want to dress up to go back
to town.

SAINT

That's right, Hagar. How much longer have you got
with us?

HAGAR

Five mont' from tomorrow, Mr. Saint.

SAINT

Are you really going back to live in town?

HAGAR

I got to, Mr. Saint.   I'se thankful for all yo' done fo' me, but I got to go to be with my baby an' to help ma raise um.

SAINT

How long since you've seen her?

HAGAR

Five mont' an' four day but she comin' tonight.

SAINT

Sure she's coming this time?

HAGAR

Yes, suh—she comin'.   Ma done promise.
    [GILLY BLUTON *enters with* DOLLY *on his arm.   He is a slim young mulatto, wearing flashy citified clothes. He walks with a swagger and makes every remark to the simple country negroes sound like an insult.   His language is halfway between Gullah and white folks' talk.* DOLLY *is young and pretty.*]

GILLY

How's everybody?

MEN

Hello, Bluton.   How yo' is, Gilly?

GILLY

                    [*Breaking in on* WHALEY.]
'Scuse me, Reverend, my purchase won't take a minute.

A cherry bounce for the lady, Davey. [DAVEY *deserts* WHALEY *to serve* GILLY. WHALEY *glares indignantly.* GILLY *hands bottle to* DOLLY.] Here you are, Baby. [*To* DAVEY.] Give me one, too, jus' for sociability.

> [DAVEY *opens second bottle for him and returns to* WHALEY. HAGAR *has moved over to the counter and is waiting patiently for* DAVEY's *attention. Her admiration is now bestowed on a huge glass jar of candy balls.* SAINT, *seeing that* WHALEY *is going to hold up traffic indefinitely, has gone back of counter to serve her.*]

SAINT

I'll get you what you want, Hagar.

HAGAR

I guess Lissa like some dese jaw-breakers.
> [*Saint opens jar. She selects them with care.*]

DOLLY

> [*Again taking* GILLY's *arm as she drinks and looking up coquettishly into his face.*]

What yo' buyin' me tonight, Honey boy?

GILLY

I told you. Anything in the store you want. Not that there's anything here worth buying. [*Turns again to* DAVEY *but* WHALEY *this time manoeuvres his broad back between them.*] Mr. Wentworth, would you be so good as to show Dolly—

SAINT

Just a minute, Bluton.   I've got a customer.

HAGAR

Gib' me t'ree of de green and six of de pink an'—

GILLY

Step on it, big gal.   Yo' think Mr. Wentworth got time for pick out your candy for yo' piece by piece?
[DOLLY *is now fingering the purple dress.*]

SAINT

[*Ignoring* GILLY]
You get seven more for a dime, Hagar.

DOLLY

I allus love dis dress.

GILLY

Ain't it too big for you?

WILLIE MAY

Do Gawd!   Here come Ned back again.

DOLLY

I mighty good at takin' t'ings in.
[SAINT *hands* HAGAR *her purchase.   Then goes into his room and closes door.   At last the* REVEREND WHALEY *departs with an overflowing basket on each arm.*]

VINA

[*Plucking* DOLLY'S *sleeve.*]

Dolly, here come yo' ole man.

DOLLY

[*Defiantly.*]

Let him come.

[NED *comes in.   Stands watching.*]

GILLY

Davey, how much this dress?

[*Takes roll of bills from pocket and leafs it over osten-
tatiously.*]

DAVEY

Four ninety-eight.   Lor', Gilly, dat's some roll yo' got!
How much yo' got dere?

GILLY

[*Laughing.*]

I got plenty.   But I can tell yo' one t'ing.   I won't have
none of it on me if I mix with you niggers this night.   I keep
my roll a place nobody'll ever find it 'cept me.   [*Pays*
DAVEY. *Hands dress to* DOLLY.]   Here you are, Baby.
When I go to Charleston tomorrow or next day I'll buy you
something worth looking at.   [*Impudently raising his
bottle.*]   How you, Ned?   Won't you join us in a cherry
bounce?   [*Drinks.   Makes wry face.*]   Beats me how all
you nigger love dis belly-wash.

NED

Give dat dress back to um, Dolly.   Yo' ain't takin' no present off other mens.

DOLLY

Now, Ned, don't yo' be gettin' so mad.   I ain't had a new dress—

NED

Yo' han' dat back.   Yo' hear what I say?

DOLLY

I hear yo' but I ain't doin' it.   Mus' be mos' a yeah since dis dress firs' come an' yo' promise um to me.   I guess I'd mebby be wearin' dis purple dress in heaben if I waits fo' yo' to buy um fo' me.

GILLY

Le's get goin', Baby.

NED

[*Seizing her arm.*]

Put dat down and come 'long home whar yo' belongs.

DOLLY

[*Shaking him off.*]

I'm a-comin' an' de dress comin' wid me.   See yo' later, honey boy.

[*Goes out with dress.. NED turns helplessly and follows.*]

GILLY

> [*Calling after them.*]

I'll be seein' yo', Baby! I'll be seein' yo', too, Ned.
Don't forget 'bout the crap game in my shack.

> [*He goes out. A moment later his car is heard leaving. SAINT comes from his room dressed for town, hands keys to DAVEY.*]

SAINT

Get my car, Davey. [DAVEY *goes out.*] Hagar, would
you put up these bolts for me?

HAGAR

Fo' sho', Mr. Saint.

> [*Begins to put heavy bolts of cloth back on shelves.*]

WILLIE MAY

> [*On porch.*]

Whar's Hagar? Here comes her ma.

> [HAGAR *tries to heave the last three bolts into place with one swing. Misses. They thud to floor.*]

HAGAR

'Scuse me, Mr. Saint.

> [*Stoops to pick up bolts.*]

MAMBA

How yo' is, Mr. Saint? I been walkin' fas', hopin' to fill
my ole eye wid de sight ob yo'.

> [HAGAR *straightens and gazes at* MAMBA *desolated.*]

SAINT

How are you, Mamba?   You didn't bring the little girl?

MAMBA

No, I ain't fotch um tonight.

HAGAR

Ma, whar's Lissa?

MAMBA

Well, yo' see, daughtuh—
[SAINT *picks up his hat.   Crosses to entrance door.*]

SAINT

Well, good night.

MAMBA

Good night, Mr. Saint.   I'm happy to see you well.
[SAINT *goes out.*]

NEGROES

[*On porch.*]
Good night, Mr. Saint.

HAGAR

Whar's Lissa?

MAMBA

[*Puffing.*]
Lemme sit down.   Dat shore is a long walk from de bus.

HAGAR

Set here, Ma. Whar's Lissa?

MAMBA

Well, daughtuh, she ain't come dis time. I sorry.

HAGAR

She ain't sick?

MAMBA

No, she ain't sick. I shore did mean fo' bring um dis time after promisin' yo' fo' five mont' now. But well, she—I guess I ain't bring that chile up to obey me like I allus done yo'. When she cry I just can't make um do t'ing.

> [Hagar's *bag of sugar balls falls open and the candies roll about on the floor. She makes no effort to pick them up and after a while the negroes pick them up and eat them.*]

HAGAR

She cry 'cause she ain't want to come?

MAMBA

Well—she went to see she ma, of course, but dey was habin' a extra choir practice dis ebenin' an' dat li'l chile do hate to miss choir practice.

HAGAR

Choir practice?

MAMBA

I ain't tell you 'bout dat yet.   [*Proudly.*]   What yo'
t'ink?   Dat gal of ours don' go to de ole East Bay Church
no more.   She go to de Reformed.

HAGAR

[*Amazed.*]
De Reformed?   Yo' mean dat big church down town?

MAMBA

Dat's de one.

HAGAR

But I—   How come she to go dar?

EVA

[*Leaning in the window.   She is dressed for church
now.*]
Dat Hagar's little gal go to de Reformed Church?   Do
Hagar?   Yo' mus' hab' mighty bright skin daughter.

HAGAR

[*Proudly.*]
I has fo' true.   My daughter brighter-skinned dan Gilly
Bluton.

MAMBA

An' she de prettiest little gal in Charleston.   An' de smart-
est.   Eberybody crazy 'bout Lissa.

HAGAR

Yo' go to de Reformed Church now, Ma?

MAMBA

Me! Lor' no! De Reformed Church no place fo' me.

EVA

I hear tell as how dey got de door of dat Reformed Church paint light tan. An' de vestrymen stan' an' watch de people come in. An' if yo' skin darker dan de door paint, why, den dey ain't got no pew fo' yo'.

MAMBA

[Laughing heartily.]
Dat's what dey do say fo' true. An' our Lissa ain't only go dere but she sing in de chillun's choir. An' de choir teacher say dere ain't nobody else can sing like Lissa.

EVA

[Turning away.]
She come natural by dat. Ain't nobody else can sing like Hagar.

HAGAR

[Worried.]
Huccum she get in dat new church, Ma?

MAMBA

Well, it's like dis. Yo' been hear me talk about a girl named Gardenia dat Lissa play wid.

HAGAR

Gardenia's dat big girl—'bout twelve or thirteen?

MAMBA

But she crazy 'bout Lissa. Gardenia's a bright skin an' all she folks is Reformed Church membuhs. An' she ax to take Lissa wid um to Sunday School. An' den dey puts Lissa in de chillun's choir. I tells yo' daughtuh, dat chile got somet'in'.

HAGAR

[*Uneasily.*]

Yo' t'ink dat good t'ing, Ma—habin' um in dat church?

MAMBA

Well, Lissa is a bright skin and we ain't.

HAGAR

I ain't want Lissa grow up ashamed of she ma an' gran'ma.

MAMBA

You leave t'ing to me. I ain't no fool at plannin' an' yo' got de strength to work fo' um. Seems lak 'tween us we ought to give our gal a chance. How yo' do dis mont'?

HAGAR

Pretty good. Here's de money. [*She takes it from front of her dress.*] It's fourteen dollah again.

MAMBA

Dat ain't so bad.

HAGAR

[*Proudly.*]

I can chop as much cotton now as any of de mens.

MAMBA

How yo' is, Sistuh Vina?

VINA

[*Who is somewhat deaf.*]

Eh? Oh, dat yo', Sistuh Mamba? Whar's de little gal?

MAMBA

I ain't could fotch um tonight.

VINA

[*Annoyed.*]

Hmph! Dat chile goin' to hab chillun 'fore Hagar eber lay an eye on um.

[*Lights her pipe.*]

MAMBA

[*Giving* VINA *her back.* To HAGAR.]

Well, if I can count on fourteen dollah ebery mont', I goin' start Lissa's music lessons.

HAGAR

Not already, Ma? She so little.

MAMBA

Certainly already. De teacher say she can start de piano now an' later on come de singin'.

[*Church bells ring out from nearby church. The light outside door and windows has faded into twilight.*]

VINA

[*Getting laboriously to her feet.*]

Guess I better be startin' fo' de church. 'Fraid I mus' be gettin' lame. Can't walk as fas' as I used to. Yo' stayin' fo' de sarvice, sistuh?

MAMBA

No. I mus' get home to Lissa. [*As the insistent bells continue, by twos and threes the negroes are leaving the porch.* It'll be black dark now 'fore I gets to town.

[VINA *hobbles out.* MAMBA *starts to rise.*]

HAGAR

[*Laying a detaining hand on her knee.*]

Don't go, Ma. Yo' ain't tol' me nuttin' yet.

MAMBA

Yo' see, daughtuh, I goin' bring um nex' time eben ef she do cry.

HAGAR

No, Ma. Don' neber do that. Don' neber bring um less she want fo' come. 'Tain't so long now. I'se on de home stretch. Some day I t'ink I can't get through de day without um. But I get through de day, an' t'rough de week an' t'rough de mont'— Come anodder five mont' an' my time is up an' I can go back to Charleston.

MAMBA

I been t'inkin' a lot about dat, daughtuh. Less dan five mont' now. Den yo' can go whar yo' likes. Charleston's a mighty big city an' full ob trouble. Here eberyt'ing is quiet an' yo' is safe. Ef yo' was to get drunk now, Lissa's big enough to know an' un'erstan'. Yo' mus' t'ink 'bout dat. An' ef yo' was to get mix up wid de police again lak yo' use to do, dat would be bery bad for Lissa. Mos' likely dey wouldn't want um no more in de Reformed Church an' dat break she heart.

HAGAR

Don't yo' worry 'bout dat, Ma. I couldn't eber do nuttin' to make Lissa 'shamed of me. I neber goin' drink anudder half pint long as I lib'. Yo' hears me promise it, Ma. An' dat's dat.

MAMBA

Did yo' know job is scarce in Charleston? It take lots of money to bring Lissa up like we's bringin' her. She can't go to de new church or to visit high class folk like Gardenia's people in ole faded dress. She got to hab t'ings new an' pretty. Here yo' got steady work an' good pay. Yo' bes' t'ink hard about dat, daughtuh, 'fore yo' makes de change.

HAGAR
[Bewildered.]
But, Ma, I gots to be in Charleston.   My little gal's dere.
*[In the nearby church the negroes begin to sing the
spiritual "I'm Goin' to Sit at de Welcome Table."]*

MAMBA
Well, we got mos' five mont' lef' fo' t'ink t'ings out.
[She gets to her feet.]   I makin' yo' late fo' church,
daughtuh.

HAGAR
[Continuing to sit and gaze into space.]
I can see um so plain some day.   Jus' lak she was standin'
dere five mont' ago.   So pretty, so sweet.   Didn't 'member
her ma bery well dough, but I don't min' when I can see
um.   But odder day I can't see um.   Dat bother me when I
can't see um.   Don't eber let nobody hurt um, Ma.

MAMBA
I ain't goin' let nobody hurt um, daughtuh.   Yo' is de one.
Don't do no more fool t'ing an' get yo'self in trouble.   Dat's
all.   *[She moves toward door.]*   Come along, I'll walk far
as de church wid yo'.

HAGAR
[Continuing to sit.]
Guess I ain't go to church tonight.

MAMBA
> [*Amazed.*]

Ain't go to church.   Yo' ain't sick, is yo'?

HAGAR

No, I jes' ain't feel like church tonight.
> [*Spiritual in church ends.*]

MAMBA
> [*Coming back to her—anxiously.*]

What de matter wid yo'?   I neber knew yo' to miss church
befo'.

HAGAR

Go 'long, Ma.   I'se all right.   It's jes' dat—I—I do miss
my baby so bad.
> [DAVEY *comes in and begins putting out lamps.*
> MAMBA *stands for a moment, uncertainly looking
> down at* HAGAR. *Then she lays a hand on her
> shoulder.*]

MAMBA

I sorry, daughtuh.   I ain't goin' to do yo' dis way again.
Good night.
> [*She goes.   The singers in church burst suddenly into
> the triumphant spiritual* "Come Out de Wilderness."
> HAGAR *sits gazing sadly before her.   But it is only a
> moment before the rhythm begins to get her.   She
> begins to sway, then to pat her hands gently.*]

SINGERS

> I'm a-leanin' on my Lord,
> I'm a-leanin' on my Lord,
> I'm a-leanin' on my Lord,
> Who died on Calvary.

[DAVEY *extinguishes last lamp, goes into* SAINT'S *room.*
HAGAR *sways faster.   Claps louder.*]

SINGERS

> An' my han' was clean
> When we come out de wilderness,
> Come out de wilderness,
> Come out de wilderness.
> An' my han' was clean
> When we come out de wilderness
> A-leanin' on my Lord.

HAGAR

[*Rising suddenly and looking up, sings with distant
choir—her burdens forgotten.*

> I'm a-leanin' on my Lord,
> I'm a-leanin' on my Lord,
> I'm a-leanin' on my Lord,
> Who died on Calvary.

[*She turns toward door.   Now that stage is dark, it can
be seen that the view beyond the door is bathed in
moonlight.   Against this in silhouette stands* HAGAR
*singing with the distant negroes as an accompani-
ment.*]

HAGAR AND CHORUS

> An' I do t'ank Gawd
> When I come out de wilderness,
> Come out de wilderness,
> Come out de wilderness.
> I do t'ank Gawd
> When I come out de wilderness
> A-leanin' on my Lord.

[*Singing she walks out into the night. And as she goes the light fades.*]

[*In the darkness between the scenes* HAGAR'S *voice grows distant, then is cut short by the sudden outburst of the Sea Island's double-clap, which beats a steady rhythm, gradually grows louder.*]

[NOTE: *This is a complicated clap indigenous to the Islands and seldom heard in the city.*]

ACT TWO

SCENE 2: *The clapping continues while lights come on revealing the interior of a negro church.*

The door is in left wall. There are windows at back. Benches for the worshippers face the pulpit.

WHALEY *is in his pulpit at right. The service is in full swing. The negroes are on their feet, clapping without song. On the floor at right front several babies are parked on a blanket asleep. For a moment the "shouting" (clapping and stamping) continues without singing. Then suddenly a high female voice raises the spiritual:*

> Tell me was yo' dar
> When we come out de wilderness,
> Come out de wilderness,
> A-leanin' on my Lord.

The whole congregation joins with a gusto that fairly shakes the church.

HAGAR *enters singing and when the next verse is reached she takes her rightful place as leader, the former leader immediately conceding her precedence.*

[NOTE: *Between verses they clap without song. In the singing of the spirituals in the low country, the leader always begins the next verse while her followers are still holding the final notes of the preceding verse.*]

70

While his flock sings WHALEY *rises and stretches out his arm to bring the spiritual to a close but for some time gets no co-operation.*

WHALEY

[*Shouting into midst of singing.*]
An' de Lord say: Hear de voice of de Lord. [*The majority grow quiet and resume seats. A few enthusiasts sing on.* WHALEY'S *sonorous voice rises above others.*] Hear de voice of de Lawd.

[*They all resume seats, panting, wiping their faces and fanning themselves.*]

WHALEY

Lissen! Believers! Las' night wid my own eyes I seen de Lawd. An' He wasn't in de city an' He wasn't on de ocean, an' He didn't wear no pressin' club cloes, an' His mouth didn't have no smooth talk. But He stan' right here on Ediwander Island an' one foot been planted at de front door of dis church an' de other foot been restin' in Combee Swamp five mile away. An' his head rise up an' bus' loose a couple of star. An' in one han' He had de sun an' in de other de moon an' He haul off—den He bring um togedder, *Blam!* An' He say—

[*A sudden violent misdirected gesture dislodges his nearly emptied flask from his tail-coat pocket and sends it clattering down on the floor to his flock's astonishment. A moment's amazed silence follows while* WHALEY *stares down at it in consternation. Then a crashing roar of laughter from the congrega-*

tion. WHALEY, *his eyes flashing, leans forward over his pulpit and his tremendous voice rises over the babblement.*]

WHALEY

An' He say, "Confess an' repent." Yo' all hear me condemn de hypocrite—enty? Yo' all hear me say, "Confess" —enty? If yo' confess an' repent w'en yo' ain't gots no reason, den yo' is hypocrite. An' God despise hypocrite worse dan rattlesnake. So now, in de presence ob dis congregation, I done t'row my licker down an' confess my sin. An' I calls on ebery brudder in dese walls for t'row he licker down. Yea, verily, if dere is one among yo' which is widout de sin ob hypocrisy, let him be de fus' to cas' he licker down. [*There is uneasy fidgeting on the benches. He quickly follows his advantage.*] Remember what de hymn say:

> Hypocrite, hypocrite God despise'
> He tongue was nibble [nimble]
> An' he will tell lies.

[*Glares down at them. None can meet his gaze. Then he snaps the tension with a thundering blow on his desk and flings his great voice into the spiritual.*]

> I ain't got no hypocrite in my heart,
> In my heart, in my heart.
> I ain't got no hypocrite in my heart.

[*His congregation quickly joins him, protectively hugging their own flasks and more than willing to let bygones be bygones.*]

I ain't got no mallets [malice] in my heart,
In my heart, in my heart.
I ain't got no mallets in my heart.

[A few singers are on their feet now. They rise as the spirit moves them, their feet slapping the floor to the rhythm.

I ain't got no cubbage [covetousness] in my heart.

Seeing his congregation absorbed, WHALEY is coming down from his pulpit to retrieve his flask when NED comes quickly forward and gets it for himself. The shouters are in full swing now. Everyone is on his feet. Halfway through each verse the steady single clap changes suddenly to the double clap. Benches are thrown back, the floor cleared.

They give themselves utterly to the rhythm. Their bodies sway and bend. Here and there two shout together, facing each other, the rest forgotten. At another place a group shout together with more concerted interplay. One woman, very old and very decrepit, shouts with the best of them, held up and sustained by a strong young female partner. But always the feet hit the same time, swaying and rattling the whole building.

Dere's a little wheel a-turnin' in my heart,
In my heart, in my heart.
Dere's a little wheel a-turnin' in my heart.

Clearly above the more measured rhythm of the spiritual with its worship of the new Christ, HAGAR's voice breaks forth into pure Gullah.]

HAGAR

> Simmi yuhba leaba simmi yuh
> Ronda bohda simmi yuh

[*Immediately they are all following her. Only the
two lines, but repeated interminably in a heavily syn-
copated rhythm with the concerted stamping of the
feet crashing through it like the thunder of a tribal
tom-tom. Women scream. Men empty their flasks
openly, their feet holding the rhythm the while.*

*The frenzied shouting surges about the room. The
babies on the floor who have at first been given a clear
berth, now seem in imminent danger, as the shouters
move relentlessly nearer. Just in the nick of time, a
shouter, scarcely losing a step, bends down and
yanks the blanket with children still sleeping to a
safer spot.*

GILLY *appears in doorway with* DOLLY *on his
arm. She is wearing the purple dress. She clings
coquettishly to him, laughing up into his face as he
derisively points out shouters he finds amusing.*

NED *stops in his shouting at left front. Glares at
them.*]

DOLLY

Come along, Gilly. Dis ain't so bad. Let's do um.

GILLY

Sure. We'll show 'em how it's done.

> [*They move down right front. Put arms around each
> other. Begin to shout.*

There is a sudden panic among the shouters as NED *is seen to whip out a razor. They scream warnings. By far the larger number escape through the door in a wild scramble. A few jump through windows. Those whose escape is cut off huddle together in corners.*

DOLLY *gives a shriek.* GILLY, *surprised, whirls about just as* NED *throws himself on him.*

There is a very brief scuffle. Then GILLY *falls to floor and* NED *dashes from church, followed by all remaining negroes.*

Faces crowd at windows looking in at GILLY *who, after a brief struggle, lies still.*]

NEGROES

[*At windows.*]

Sweet Jedus! He done done fo' um. T'ank Gawd we shut of dat dirty yaller houn'.

Sarves um right.

Gawd how dat nigger bleed.

HAGAR

[*In window.*]

Mebbe he ain't daid.

DRAYTON

He daid soon all right. All we gots to do is leab' um be.

[HAGAR *withdraws from window and a second later enters door. Runs to* GILLY. *Bends over him.*]

HAGAR

He ain't daid. Somebody help me quick. He bleedin'
like a ribber.

VOICES

Let um be. Come away.

HAGAR

Gimme han', somebody. He goin' fas'. Can't be yo' goin'
stan' dere an' let a man daid. [*Nobody speaks nor moves.*
HAGAR *hoists skirt and snatches off petticoat. Tears it into*
strips.] Help me, somebody. Dis nigger goin' fas'.

MINGO

Come away, you fool. Let dat gambler be.
    [*Working with frantic haste,* HAGAR *binds wounds.*
    Then straightens up and looks toward watchers in
    windows. Their number has diminished but a few
    faces still stare in.]

HAGAR

We gots to get um to town quick. If we can get um to
de hospital, mebbe dey can pull um t'rough. [*Complete*
silence from watchers. Nobody moves. HAGAR *crosses sud-*
denly to window. Seizes old DRAYTON *by arm.*] You lissen
to me. I done seen yo' wagon hitch down de road. You git
it here soon as yo' can.

DRAYTON

[*Pulling away.*]
Lemme be, sistuh. Dat Gawd dam son of a bitch can't
daid too quick to suit me.

HAGAR

If dat wagon ain't here in five minute' I goin' run yo' off
dis plantation.   Onnerstan'?

DRAYTON

Mebbe I'll get de wagon fo' yo' but I ain't goin' drive um
to de hospital.

[He goes.]

HAGAR

[Returning to bandaging.]
Ain't dere nobody here'll drive dis man to de hospital
'fore he dies?

MINGO

Dat ain't no use.   Dey ain't lets nuttin' but city niggers
free to de hospital.   Country niggers got to pay in exwance.

HAGAR

Dat all right.   Gilly allus gots money.   *[Goes through
his pockets.]*   Nuttin' in dis pocket.   None here.   Do Lor'!
He ain't got a cent on um.

DAVEY

[Laughing loudly.]
Ain't we hear him say he ain't goin' to have none on him
if he mix wid us tonight?

[Raucous laughter at all windows.]

MINGO

Serve' um right.   Can't trust we.   Now he can daid.

WILLIE MAY

Ain't nuttin' but a low double-crossin' nigger anyhow.

HAGAR

He ain't goin' daid. Yo' hear dat, yo' dirty passel of yaller-liver' nigger. He ain't goin' daid. 'Cause one of yo' mens is goin' drive de wagon to Charleston and get um in de hospital whedder we can pay fo' um or not.

MINGO

Yeah? Who goin' to do dat, sistuh? Firs' t'ing dey wants to know is, who cut um. An' de only pusson dey can lay dey han' on is de one what drive um to de hospital.

HAGAR

Lissen, I tell yo' what we gots to do. Somebody goin' drive um to de city an' take um near de hospital. Den when nobody's lookin' lift um out de wagon an' leave um on de pavement whar he's sure to be foun'. Den dey t'ink he's a Charleston nigger an' take um in to de hospital. Ain't one of you mens do dat?

EVA

What you want to save um for so bad? You ain't los' your haid ober um like half the young gal 'roun' here, is yo'?

HAGAR

He ain't a Gawd's t'ing to me. It jes' don't come natural to me to let a man daid wid no one to help um.

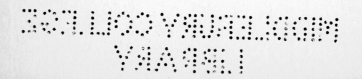

MINGO

Den help um yo'self, sistuh.   If yo' wants um driv' to town so bad, drive um yo'self.

[*Rattle of wagon is heard, as it draws up and stops at door.*]

DRAYTON

[*Outside.*]

Here yo' is, sistuh.   I do like yo' tell me an' dat's all I'm doin'.

HAGAR

You wouldn't drive um, Drayton?

DRAYTON

Not on yo' life.

HAGAR

Davey!   [DAVEY *only laughs.*]   Mingo, you ain't 'fraid of nuttin', big mans like yo'.

MINGO

I not 'fraid of nuttin' 'cept dat Gilly Bluton ain't goin' to daid.

[HAGAR *straightens and faces window.*]

HAGAR

Yo' damned rotten low-livered niggers.   Yo' fair mek me 'shamed to be black.   [*Strides to door.*]   Back yo' wagon to de do'.   I drivin' um to town myself.

[*Quick black-out.*]

ACT TWO

SCENE 3: MAMBA's *room.* *It is the same room as of Act One, Scene 1. Even now it is not a typical negro room in that it is not cluttered with odds and ends. It is very neat and the window is open.*

The room is dark, the only illumination being a kerosene lamp turned very low. MAMBA is asleep on the bed.

A knock.

HAGAR'S VOICE
Ma! Ma!

MAMBA
 [*Raising up.*]
Who's dar?

HAGAR
Ma, it's Hagar. Lemme in.

MAMBA
 [*Getting up quickly.*]
Do Gawd! [*Crosses to door.*] Dat yo', Hagar?

HAGAR
Let me in quick, Ma.
 [MAMBA *unlocks and opens door.* HAGAR *goes quickly in.*]

MAMBA

For Gawd's sake, daughtuh, why you here? [HAGAR
quickly shuts door behind her. Leans against it.] What yo'
doin' in town? [MAMBA *turns up lamp. In the light she
scrutinizes* HAGAR.] Yo' all right, gal? Yo' ain't sick?

HAGAR

[*Breathless.*]

No, I had to come. A man was dyin'. Nobody else
would take um to the hospital. I ain't know if I got um
dere in time.

MAMBA

What yo' talkin' about? What man?

HAGAR

I ain't got time to tell yo' all about dat. The police goin'
to get me. I come fo' see Lissa.

MAMBA

De police after you? [HAGAR *nods.*] An' yo' come here
whar dey goin' look fo' yo' first.

HAGAR

It ain't matter where I go, Ma. Dey knows I's in town
an' I can't get out. All dey's got to do is to watch de bridge
till dey catch me.

MAMBA

How yo' know de police seen yo'?

HAGAR

He seen me plain. He say, "Well, if it ain't de big un back in town." Den I 'members my time ain't up an' I knows dey's goin' get me, so I whip up de horse an' come here to see Lissa. Where she is, Ma?

MAMBA

Whar yo' t'ink she is at this time of night? In she bed asleep.

HAGAR

[*Crossing toward* LISSA's *door.*]
I got to see um.

MAMBA

No, not now. We got to think. We got to get yo' away.

HAGAR

[*Turning near door.*]
Ma, yo' know I can't go back across de bridge and dere's no other way to go. Dey goin' to put me up fo' five yeah. Five yeah I won't see my little gal. I *got to* see um.

MAMBA

Oh, Gawd, Gawd! Why yo' gots to saddle me wid dis pure fool?
[*In impotent rage she pursues and seizes* HAGAR *and tries to shake her. She is so much smaller that though* HAGAR *is submissive, she shakes herself.*]

HAGAR

[*Almost sobbing.*]

Don't, Ma! I know I bin a fool. I ain't t'ink. Please let me see Lissa.

MAMBA

Lemme wake um. She might feel strange waked in de night by someone she ain't know so well. [MAMBA *goes into* LISSA's *room.* HAGAR *crosses to left and faces door. A moment later* MAMBA *returns, pushing ahead of her a very sleepy child.* HAGAR *drops on one knee and holds out her arms.* MAMBA *pushes the child toward her.* HAGAR *clasps it to her. For one passive moment the child waits, then squirms and frees itself. Returns to* MAMBA.] Go kiss yo' ma, chile; she got to go 'way.

[*The child continues to lean against* MAMBA, *who urges her toward* HAGAR. *The child whispers to* MAMBA.]

HAGAR

What she say?

MAMBA

[*With embarrassed laugh.*]

Don't mind, daughtuh. I bring dis chile up different from you. Since I been workin' wid white folks I see how de white chillun is raised an' I gib dis chile a bath ebery day.

HAGAR

Ebery day! You t'ink dat good fo' um?

MAMBA

Don' hurt white chillun none.   An' dat's huccum she don'
hab none of dose good homey smells yo' had when yo' was
a chile.   An' she ain't used to um.   Go 'long.   Kiss yo' ma.
It's jus' good hard work makes 'em smell dat way.   [*The
child reluctantly approaches* HAGAR, *who does not again try
to detain her.   She gives* HAGAR *a swift kiss and goes back to*
MAMBA.]   Don't yo' mind um, daughtuh.   She jus' feel a
little strange wid yo' at first.
> [*She sits in chair at right and takes the child on her lap.*
> HAGAR *looks about her uncertainly.*]

HAGAR

Eberyt'ing so different.   I hardly knows where I am at.
Mos' like white pusson's home.   Look, Ma, huccum yo' got
de window up?   Yo' ain't 'fraid Lissa's catch cold?
> [*Crosses to close window.*]

MAMBA

Lef' um.   My white folks say it's good fo' chillun.

HAGAR

> [*Doubtfully.*]

Might be good for white chillun— [*Looks uneasily at the
tidy furniture.*]   Where can I set, Ma?   Dis all right?
> [*Chooses rocking chair at left facing* MAMBA.]

MAMBA

Yes, set down.   We gots to mek plans.   Mebbe I could
hide yo' out somewheres for few days.

HAGAR

'Tain't no use. De cops know me too well. I's too big.
Dey neber forget me. Lissen, Ma. I got to tell you 'bout
de wagon. I hitched um in Elliot Street near de corner of
South Bay. You'll hab to get a boy to drive um back. It's
all bloody, so it will hab to be washed good or somebody else
might be gettin' into trouble.

MAMBA

[*Rocking child.*]
Who de debil is dis man yo' do all dis fo'? He yo' man?

HAGAR

Yo' knows I got no man. It's jus' dat he was bleedin' to
deat' an' nobody else'd help um. I ain't t'ink. I was t'inkin'
so hard 'bout gettin' um to de hospital I forgot all 'bout my
time ain't up an' I ain't got no right to come to town an' I
ain't 'membuh till de cop see me.

MAMBA

Whar he see yo'?

HAGAR

Near de hospital. I drive near de hospital and I lift
Gilly Bluton out an' lay um on de sidewalk. Den I drive
de wagon a little ways off an' hitch um in de dark at de side
of de road. Den I creep back an' watch to see if dey get
Gilly all right. An' pretty soon somebody come along an'
see Gilly an' gib de alarm——

MAMBA

Gilly?   Yo' mean dat yaller woman-chasin' gambler?

HAGAR

Yes, dat's de one.

MAMBA

Do Gawd!

HAGAR

Den I slip back to de wagon an' onhitch um an' get aboard. But I see somebody was comin' along down de sidewalk, so I sets quiet in de dark.   Den I see it was de cop on his beat but I sets quiet.   But he sees dere's somet'in' dar an' he flash a flashlight in my face an' he say, "If it ain't de big un!" An' wid dat I whip up dat horse and drive fas' an' lef' um standin' dere an' I come here fo' see my baby 'cause I ain't goin' see um again fo' five yeah.   Look, she's asleep already. [*Crosses and looks down at* LISSA.]   She wouldn't know now if I was to take um.

   [*Gently takes the sleeping child and returns to rocking chair.   Rocks the child.*]

MAMBA

[*Sadly.*]

Eberyt'ing was goin' fine.   I tell all Lissa's fine frien' as how her ma had good job in de islands an' sen' her money regular.   Now eberybody goin' to hear how her ma is a jailbird.

HAGAR

No, Ma. Nobody needs hear about um. Eberyt'ing goin'
be jus' de same for Lissa 'cept fo' de money. Yo' got to
mek money now, Ma, den when I gets out I goin' work twice
as hard for um. [*Realizing it for first time.*] I guess I
neber come back to Charleston now. Yo' right. I too big
a fool fo' de city. I'll go back to de plantation when I come
out of jail. Dat'll be jus' five yeah. Lissa will be a big gal,
gettin' on wid her music lesson an' t'ing.

MAMBA

You blunderin' fool. Why yo' gots to do dis t'ing?

HAGAR

You mus' neber bring um to de jail, Ma, or tell um one
Gawd's t'ing about me. I thought dat cop'd be here 'fore
now. [*Looks from window in which a red light is growing.
Gets up to carry child near window.*] Ain't nobody down
dere yet. [*Looking out at dawn she draws a deep breath.*]
Oh, Gawd, in a worl' like dis, why yo' gots to make me such
a damned fool? I mos' forgot how de sun looks comin' up
out of de water back of Fort Sumter.

MAMBA

[*Suddenly.*]
De water! Do gal! Yo' ain't de only fool! Huccum I
ain't t'ink of dat! Dere's de water.

HAGAR

De—what?

MAMBA

[Getting to her feet.]

Ediwander's a island, enty?   He got water around um,
well as a bridge, enty?   Yo' gots to go across de water.

HAGAR

How I do dat?   I can't swim um.

MAMBA

Yo' hear of such t'ing as a boat, ain't yo'?   Tim Hardy he
got a boat.   It ain't goin' to be full light for anodder hour.
[HAGAR *again sits with the child.*]   Get up, gal.   Don't be
a-settin' down.   Yo' got to get out of here 'fore de cops fin'
yo'.   No—lemme see—I ain't want yo' traipsin' 'roun' with
me.   You wait here.   I'll go ask Tim an' persuade him an'
fin' jus' whar de boat's at.   Den while he gettin' de boat
ready I'll sen' his boy Neddy back to tell you whar to meet
him.

HAGAR

[Doubtfully.]

Yo' t'ink he'll want to take a chance?

MAMBA

He'll take a chance if I pay him enough.   Put dat chile
back in its bed and be ready when Neddy comes for you.   It
won't be more'n a few minute.   [MAMBA *goes to door. Is
arrested by a thought. Returns to* HAGAR.]   An' if dat
police does get here befo' Neddy—'membuh—*keep yo'
mout' shut*—or dey'll be pinnin' de Bluton cuttin' on yo'
too.   'Membuh dat now.

HAGAR

Yes, Ma. I'll 'membuh dat. I'm to keep um shut.

[MAMBA *starts to open door. Then with brief spurt of tenderness returns to* HAGAR. *Lays hand on arm.*]

MAMBA

I mebbe won't see you again. Good-bye, daughtuh. De Lawd bless yo' an' pertect yo' an' keep yo' f'om bein' such a Gawd-damned fool.

[*She goes.* HAGAR *continues to rock the child. After a moment she begins to hum "Motherless Children," raises the little head and lays it more comfortably against her breast. Begins to sing in a low voice. Little by little her voice increases in volume but holds a lullaby cadence. A heavy step on stair. Then a knock at the door.* HAGAR *rises quickly, holding child to her breast, looking at the closed door. The knock is repeated. The door is pushed open revealing a policeman standing there. He wears an expression of reluctance. Quickly.*]

HAGAR

All right, I's a-comin'.

[*Continues to sing in low tone. Carries child into her room. Within the room she begins to hum. Returns immediately and does not cease to hum soothingly until she has softly closed the bedroom door. Then she straightens, walks rapidly to the door where policeman waits, goes out and closes it behind her.*]

CURTAIN

ACT THREE

ACT THREE

SCENE 1: *The store three years ago. It is little changed from the old days.* DAVEY, *no longer a boy, is back of the counter. The negroes of the previous scenes are there, making purchases and gossiping together. Some of the younger generation are mixing among them.*

SAINT, *his hair now gray, sits at his desk.*

HAGAR *enters in a bright, new dress. The years have made little change in her. At present she is looking excited and happy.*

She stands by SAINT's *desk, waiting for his attention.*

SAINT

Want something, Hagar? [*Then he looks up at her.*] Well, you've got it on!

HAGAR

[*Delighted.*]

How it look, Mr. Saint?

SAINT

Great.

HAGAR

[*Wriggling uncomfortably in it.*]

It's little bit tight but it's goin' to be all right jus' fo' to-night. Seems like they make all de dresses fo' puny little women. Now, I want something else.

SAINT

Don't tell me you want a hat!   I couldn't stand it to have you go haywire after all these years.

HAGAR

No, Mr. Saint.   I ain't need no hat.   I want my money.

SAINT

How much of it do you want?

HAGAR
All of it.

SAINT

All of it?   [*Leaning back in his chair and looking up at her.*]   So the great day has come.

HAGAR

[*Happily.*]

Yes, suh.

SAINT

[*Getting down and opening a ledger.*]
You're going to send her to New York?

HAGAR

Yes, suh.   In 'bout a mont'—   Jus' as soon as we can fin' somebody goin' dat'll take care of um on de train an' fin' a place fo' um in New York dat's safe fo' young cullud gal.

SAINT

You've got a lot of money here, Hagar.   Are you sure you want it all?

HAGAR

Yes, suh.   Ma's comin' fo' it tonight.   She's got to get Lissa ready.   Buy clothes an' t'ing.   [*Importantly.*]   Lissa's comin' too.

SAINT

[*Smiling.*]

So that's the reason for the big dressing up!   [*A little worried.*]   Sure she's going to show up this time?

HAGAR

Yes, suh, Mr. Saint.   She's comin' fo' sure.   Ma sen' me word by Davey.   Lissa's goin' to a dance at dat road house on de Ediwander Road—Upjack's, dey calls um.   Couple of boys are takin' she an' she girl frien'.   Dey come within five mile of here, so Lissa's gettin' the boys to drive she an' Ma up here so I can see um.

SAINT

Now look here, Hagar.   [*Shows book.*]   Since you began banking with me—these are the figures.   This is what you've put in each week.

HAGAR

Yo' know I ain't can read um, Mr. Saint.

SAINT

Well, it comes to eight hundred and forty-nine dollars and
nineteen cents. [*To himself—a little sadly.*] Eight hundred and forty-nine dollars and nineteen cents.

HAGAR

[*Waits.   Puzzled by his expression.*]
Is somet'ing wrong, Mr. Saint?

SAINT

[*Shaking head and smiling at her.*]
I've just been trying to realize it.   Though we've been
here together all these years—except for the five years you
were away—and I've been watching you, living on next to
nothing, never a pretty dress till tonight—I can hardly make
out how you've done it.   If that girl of yours ever lets you
and Mamba down I'll want to wring her neck.   [*Resuming
businesslike tone.*] You understand that I haven't the money
here for you.   It's in the bank in town.   But I can write a
check for the money which you must sign.

[*While* SAINT *is explaining procedure to* HAGAR,
GILLY's *car is heard stopping outside.   It is evidently
a new car.   The negroes on porch admire it.*]

VOICES

Ain't dat some car!
Did you see dat new car Gilly got?   Sho' some auto.

[GILLY *goes in.   He has changed from a flashily
dressed youth to a man in early middle age whose
clothes, though extreme in cut, are apparently made*

*by a good tailor. But he still has the insolent manner
and the swagger. His face is marked by a scar.*]

SAINT

[*Writing as he talks.*]

Mamba must take this to the bank on Broad Street. She
must sign it on the back and they will give her the money.

GILLY

[*Turning in doorway.*]

Say, you niggers. Keep your hands off that car. You
think I want it all smeared up by your dirty hands? [*Swaggers in. Greeted with no enthusiasm except by one young
girl.*]

MARTHA

Hello, Gilly.

GILLY

[*Not interested.*]

'Lo, Martha.

[*She beckons* GILLY *over and he saunters indolently
up.*]

MARTHA

Want to see me later, honey?

GILLY

[*Indifferently.*]

Oh, I reckon so.

MARTHA

I'll slip over to your shack soon as I can make it.

[GILLY *crosses to counter. Becomes the center of a group right back.*]

SAINT

Here you are. [*Reads.*] Pay to the order of Mamba Wentworth eight hundred and forty-nine dollars and nineteen cents. Signed Hagar Wentworth. Put your X here.

[HAGAR *makes cross. There is loud talking and scuffling from* GILLY'S *group.* SAINT *looks up quickly. Noting his observation, the group calms down.*]

HAGAR

I t'ank yo' kindly, Mr. Saint.

SAINT

[*Closing the book and rising.*]

Don't lose it, Hagar.

HAGAR

Yo' ain't goin' right away, is yo', Mr. Saint? I does want yo' to see—I does want Lissa to see yo'.

SAINT

I want to see her, too. No, I'm not going immediately.

[*Crosses to his room. Goes in and closes door. The closing of* SAINT'S *door is signal for the argument to break out again.*]

HAGAR

[*To* WILLIE MAY.]
Has yo' hear my daughter comin' to see me tonight?

WILLIE MAY

Well, now, you don' say!
[MAUM' VINA *hobbles in, a very old woman now.*
MARTHA *is sitting on her keg, her mind on attracting*
GILLY'S *attention.*]

EVA

[*Peremptorily.*]
Here's Maum' Vina, gal.
[MARTHA *looks annoyed but gets to her feet.* VINA
*indicates by an imperious gesture that the keg should
be further to the right. The girl obediently tries to
move it. She is a slim young thing and the keg is
apparently very heavy.* HAGAR, *seeing her difficulty,
crosses and lifts the keg easily to its accustomed spot.
As she does so a car stops outside.* HAGAR *glances up
quickly.*]

VINA

[*Detaining her.*]
Hold my stick, daughter. [HAGAR *obediently takes it.*]
Now let me down easy. [HAGAR *assists her to seat.*] When's
your gal comin'?

HAGAR

Might be dat's she now.
[*Starts toward door.*]

VINA

[*Who has now grown very deaf, pulling her back by dress.*]

What you say?

HAGAR

[*Shouting in her ear.*]

I t'ink mebby she comin' now.

VINA

[*Still detaining her.*]

Eh?

HAGAR

Just a minute, Mauma.

[MAMBA *comes in.* *She looks much older and is far less spry.* GARDENIA *and* TONY *appear in doorway. They stand waiting for their companions.*]

MAMBA

Good evenin'.

NEGROES

Good ebenin', Maum' Mamba.

[*She crosses to* HAGAR *and* VINA.]

MAMBA

Well, daughtuh, how yo' is?

[*Kisses her.*]

HAGAR

How yo' is, Ma?

[Her eyes quickly revert to door. She is excited and happy but a little frightened lest she do the wrong thing.

All eyes are on GARDENIA *who wears a showy, tight-fitting evening dress. As always, she is good-natured, flamboyant. The negroes stand silently to the sides of the room, gazing upon her as something strange and new. Her escort* TONY *is a slight, well-dressed young negro.* MAMBA *is greeting* VINA.*]*

MAMBA

I glad fo' see yo' well, Sistuh.

VINA

How yo' is, Sistuh?

EVA

Dat yo' daughter, Hagar?
            *[*HAGAR *shakes head.]*

MAMBA

Come here, Gardenia. Dis Lissa's mother.

GARDENIA

            [Going to HAGAR *and shaking hands.]*
I shore am glad meet you.

HAGAR

T'ank yo' kindly, Miss Gardenia.
    [But she has eyes only for the door. LISSA *appears in*

*the doorway and momentarily hesitates there, look-
ing for her mother. She is charming; young and
slender with ivory skin. Everything about her is of
the latest fashion—her evening dress, her slippers,
her evening bag, the way she wears her hair. But
she is not a happy-looking girl. At times she talks
and laughs with animation but when in repose her
face is strained, discontented. Though scrupulously
polite, undoubtedly she feels superior to her sur-
roundings.*

The negroes stare in silent admiration. GILLY,
*looking her over, expresses his surprise in a low whis-
tle, seats himself on counter at right back, takes out
and lights cigarette. He scarcely takes his eyes off
her during the rest of the scene.*

LISSA *sees* HAGAR *and crosses quickly to her.*
HAGAR, *her eyes shining with happiness, seems rooted
to the spot.*]

LISSA

Mother, I'm so glad to see you.

[HAGAR *is a little uncertain what greeting will be well
received. So she waits for* LISSA *to make the first
move.* LISSA *gives her a polite kiss.* HAGAR, *deeply
gratified, returns the kiss with restrained ardor. Then
gazes at* LISSA *with wondering admiration.*]

HAGAR

My little gal! Yo' so beautiful! [*To the admiring
crowd.*] Do Gawd! T'ink of me havin' a daughtuh like
dat.

LISSA
> [*Laughing, embarrassed.*]

Mother! Don't! You'll make me conceited.

MAMBA

Here's Maum' Vina.
> [LISSA *politely bends down to shake hands with the old*
> *woman.*]

VINA

How yo' is, gal? Yo' mighty pretty.

LISSA

Oh, thank you.

VINA

I hears yo' got a mighty purty voice too. I ain't can hear um so good dese day. Yo' ma countin' a lot on yo'. Now don't yo' go an' disappoint um.

LISSA

I'll try not to.

VINA

What yo' say?

MAMBA

Yo' got to yell at um, Lissa.

LISSA

[Shouting in her ear.]

I'll try not to. [VINA *nods approval. The two escorts*
have followed LISSA.] Mother, may I present Mr. Endicott?

HAGAR

[Shaking hands with SLIM.]

How yo' is, Mr. Endicott.

LISSA

And Mr. Reed.

TONY

[Shaking hands with HAGAR.]

Glad to meet yo'.

HAGAR

T'ank yo' kindly. [EVA *and* WILLIE MAY *have pressed
in, waiting to meet* LISSA. SLIM *and* TONY *join* GARDENIA.
Proudly.] *Mis'* Flood, meet Lissa. Lissa, dis Mis' Flood.

EVA

I proud fo' meet yo', Miss Wentworth. We all hear yo'
sing las' week over Mr. Saint's radio.

WILLIE MAY

Yo' shore sing good.

[As the introductions take place, GARDENIA *at right
front has spied* GILLY, *to whom* MARTHA *is talking.*

He is nodding occasionally in answer but keeps his eyes on Lissa.]

GARDENIA

Do Lor', if it isn't the Prince himself!

GILLY

Hello, Gardenia.

[*He gets off counter with deliberation and walks out on* Martha *without a glance. Saunters down to* Gardenia. *The negroes at left surrounding* Lissa, *their backs to audience, make the conversation in that quarter unintelligible to the audience.*]

SLIM

Hello, Prince.

GILLY

Hello, Slim.

TONY

Hey, Prince.

GARDENIA

What in the world are you doin' here?

GILLY

I live down here. [*With a meaning look.*] Now who'd 've thought you'd forgotten that?

GARDENIA
[*Slightly annoyed.*]
I do remember you lived somewhere on Ediwander.

GILLY
[*Indicating* LISSA.]
Where'd you get her?

GARDENIA
Oh, Lissa.   We're old friends.   Where you been keepin'
yourself?   Used to see you at Upjack's nearly every night.

GILLY
You goin' there tonight?

GARDENIA
Yes.

GILLY
She goin' too?

GARDENIA
Sho', we're all going.   They got Ronnie Bolton and his
orchestra.

MAMBA
Mr. Saint gone?   I wanted um to see Lissa.

HAGAR
He ain't gone yet.   I'll tell um.
[*Crosses to* SAINT's *door and knocks.*]

SAINT

[Within room.]

Yes?

HAGAR

Mr. Saint, I want my daughter fo' meet you.

SAINT

[Coming from room, dressed for town.]
I want to meet your daughter, too.

HAGAR

[Proudly.]

Mr. Saint, dis she.

SAINT

So this is Lissa.

LISSA

[Politely, as though speaking to an equal.]
How do you do, Mr. Saint.

MAMBA

[In a low tone.]
Drap curtsy, gal. *[*LISSA *looks discomfited, slightly annoyed.* SAINT *crosses to her.]* 'Scuse it, Mr. Saint. Dese young folks ain't got de ole-time manners.

SAINT

Times are changing, Mamba. *[Shakes hands with* LISSA. *Looks at her searchingly.]* How do you do, Lissa. I'm very glad to see you. I have been wondering for a long time what the object of all this devotion would be like.

LISSA

[*Discomfited.*]
What—I beg your pardon, Mr. Saint?

HAGAR

[*Proudly.*]
Mr. Saint was listening to you, Lissa, both time you sing on the Charleston radio. He say you sing very nice.

LISSA

Thank you, Mr. Saint, I'm awfully glad that you liked it.

SAINT

I did and you certainly come by it naturally. Some day you must get your mother to teach you my favorite song. [LISSA *seems taken aback by suggestion that her mother could teach her anything.* SAINT *picks up his hat from desk. Turns back to* LISSA.] Your mother tells me that you will be off to New York in a few weeks. I wish you the very greatest success. You aren't going to expect it to be easy?

LISSA

Oh, no, Mr. Saint. I know I have got a lot to learn. I'm going to work awfully hard.

SAINT

That's right. Don't let us down. Good-bye and good luck. I'm off now, Hagar.

HAGAR

Very well, Mr. Saint. I'll see to everything.

MAMBA

Good night, Mr. Saint.

SAINT

Good night, Mamba. [*To room in general.*] Good night.

NEGROES

Good night, Mr. Saint.

[*He goes.*]

HAGAR

[*To* MAMBA.]

De store break into couple of time when Mr. Saint been away. I sleep in um now when he goes to town. I'm de night watcherman.

[MARTHA *and several other young people have joined the group at right and are talking to* GARDENIA *and* TONY. SLIM *hovers around* LISSA. GILLY *returns to his place on counter with his inevitable cigarette.* HAGAR *goes to get chair which is just in front of* GILLY.]

GILLY

Some daughter, big gal!

HAGAR

[*Proudly.*]

She shore is.

GILLY

Introduce me.

HAGAR

[*Shaking head.*]

Yo' ain't want to meet um.   She ain't yo' kin'.   My daughtuh's a good gal.

GILLY

You telling *me*?   I'll say she's good.

[HAGAR *gives him no further attention.   Carries her chair over to sit by* MAMBA *and* VINA.   LISSA *is eager to question her mother but* EVA *takes her arm and propels her toward the group of young people.*]

EVA

Come meet my gal, Martha.

[*Introduces her.*]

MAMBA

[*To* HAGAR.]

Yo' sleepin' here?   Where I goin' to sleep?

HAGAR

[*Pleased.*]

You fixin' to spen' the night here?

MAMBA

Yo' ain't t'ink I'd be goin' to a dance, is yo'?   I fixin' to spen' the night an' take de early mornin' bus.   Lissa's sleepin' at Gardenia's.

HAGAR

That's fine, Ma.   I'll make you comfortable.   I've got a roll of bedding dere [*points back of stove*] to spread on the floor fo' yo'.   I can sleep fine in that big chair.

SLIM

[*Taking out cigarette, elaborately to* HAGAR.]
May I smoke, Mrs. Wentworth?

HAGAR

[*Astonished.*]
What yo' ax me?

SLIM

May I smoke?

HAGAR

Fo' shore yo' may.   [SLIM *rejoins the group of young people.*   HAGAR *takes out her pipe and looks at it.   Then looks around the room uneasily.   Her eye lights on the other escort and she calls.*]   Mr. Endicott— Oh, Mr. Endicott.   [*He looks around, surprised.   Holding out her pipe and imitating* SLIM's *manner.*]   May I smoke, Mr. Endicott?

[*She is not being funny but trying to practice good manners.   He nods a surprised assent.*   HAGAR *lights pipe.*   GARDENIA *crosses toward* MAMBA *and* HAGAR.]

HAGAR
[To MAMBA.*]*
Yo' are shore this Upjack's is an all right place for Lissa
to go?   They talks sort of funny about um roun' here.

MAMBA
I ain' want um to go but Gardenia say it's all right.
[Looking up affectionately at GARDENIA *as she approaches.]*
I ain' worry 'bout Lissa when she's with Gardenia.

GARDENIA
[Sitting on floor at their feet.]
That's right, Grandma.   It would be a shame to keep
Lissa from dancing.   She's the best dancer in Charleston.
[To HAGAR.*]*   Don't you worry.   It's not a place I'd want
her to go myself if I weren't along.   Nobody's going to get
fresh with Lissa when I'm with her.   I've looked on Lissa
like she was my little sister since she was four years old.

HAGAR
I knows I can trus' yo'.   Yo're a good gal.

GARDENIA
You're right.   You can trust me.   Maybe I ain't what
some folks mean by a good girl.   But Lissa is and I'm go-
ing to see that she stays that way.
*[*LISSA *returns to her mother.]*
LISSA
Mother, what was it Mr. Saint meant about your teaching
me his favorite song?
*[*HAGAR *and* MAMBA *both very much embarrassed.]*

MAMBA

Don' worry yo' ma now; she ain't got no time fo' sing.

HAGAR

An' I can't sing nohow. Le's talk 'bout somet'ing else.

EVA

Don't yo' believe um. Make um sing "Lonesome Walls."

OTHER NEGROES

Yes. Come on. Hagar, sing um.

HAGAR

[*Showing anger and almost in tears.*]
Shut up, all of you. Lef' me an' my gal alone.

MAMBA

[*To* LISSA.]
Don' lissen to 'em, gal.

LISSA

Why, what's the matter? What song is this anyway?

MARTHA

It's dat jail house song Hagar bring back wid um.
[*There is instant silence, everyone realizing too late what a blunder has been made.* HAGAR *is sitting with her face in her hands.*]

LISSA

[*Drawing back.*]
Oh! [*After a moment she leans forward and puts her*

hand on HAGAR's *knee, then says gently:*] Please sing it
for me, Mother—dear.

> [HAGAR *commences to sing with her face in her hands.
> As she sings she drops first one hand and then the
> other and sits looking beyond the circle, having for-
> gotten where she is. The song should emerge casu-
> ally, in the folk manner, and should start almost
> upon a conversational note.*]

HAGAR

[*Speaking.*]
You all 'member my man?

PEOPLE

[*Speaking.*]
Yes, Sistuh, we 'members yo' man.

HAGAR

[*Beginning to sing.*]
Well, my man told me when dey took me away
Dat he would come to see me every Chris'mus Day,
Now Chris'mus is over, an' dey's lockin' de gate—
[*Pleadingly.*]
Oh, Mister Jailer, please wait—'tain't late!
[*Sadly, with resignation.*]
No use waitin', watchin', hopin', for a man who forgets you,
      an' ain't willin' to wait.
Dere's too many women for a man to wait.

CHORUS

[With nostalgic longing.]

Mornin', is you still bornin' de clean young day?
River, is you still talkin' where my chillun play?
Stars, is you still shinin' when evenin' falls
While my heart's pinin' deep in dese lonesome walls?
Lonesome walls, lonesome walls, deep in dese lonesome
    walls.

HAGAR

[Speaking.]

You all 'member my boy Jessie?

PEOPLE

[Speaking.]

Yes, Sistuh, we 'members yo' boy.

HAGAR

[Beginning to sing.]

My boy was straight until he traveled to town,
But women an' de licker an' de bones got him down.
An' now de jail barber is a-shavin' his hair—
[Pleadingly.]
Oh, Mister Whiteman, take care—he's dear!
While Death's waitin' in de death-house always hungry an'
    a-dustin' off his terrible chair,
Beckonin' an' bowin' by his big black chair.

    *[HAGAR repeats chorus while people, one by one, begin
    to hum in chorus.]*

HAGAR

[*Speaking.*]

You all ain't forgotten Hagar, is you.

PEOPLE

[*Speaking.*]

No, Sistuh, we ain't forgot Hagar.

HAGAR

[*Beginning to sing.   On an exultant note.*]

One of dese mornin's if I'm livin' day long
I'm goin' to rise up singin' such a good-bye song
Dat walls will fly open to de sky an' de sea—
[*With ecstasy.*]
Oh, Mister Jailer, can't be—I'm free!
Den I'll travel always singin' to my home where tomorrow
    is a-waitin' for me.
There's still a tomorrow waitin' there for me.

[*Chorus, with people joining full voice.   When the
    music ceases* LISSA *has tears in her eyes.   She goes
    to her mother and kisses her.   Says nothing.   There
    is the sound of an auto horn outside.*]

SLIM

[*Coming down to* GARDENIA *and* LISSA.]

Say, it's time to get goin' the dance done started.   [*To*
HAGAR.]   Good night, Mrs. Wentworth.   [*Shakes hands.*]

GARDENIA

Good night, Mrs. Wentworth.   So glad to have met you.
[*Pats* MAMBA *on the shoulder.*]   See you tomorrow,

Grandma. [*Takes* SLIM'S *arm and starts toward the door.*]
We'll wait for you outside, Lissa.

LISSA

I'll be right there.
[GILLY *gets off counter, saunters toward door.*]

MARTHA
[*Following him.*]
Hey, Gilly, yo' ain't fergittin' 'bout tonight? See you
later.

GILLY

That's off. Fergit it.

MARTHA

Oh, honey! What yo' means?

GILLY

Fergit it. I got other fish to fry.
[*Saunters out.*]

LISSA

I'll see you again before I go, Mother. Slim will drive
me out any time I say.

MAMBA

Den I comin' wid yo'. I ain't let yo' drive way out here
all by yo'self wid that slippery-looking feller.

LISSA
[*With amused affection.*]
All right, Grandma, I'll be delighted to have you.

[*A car heard departing.* LISSA, *startled, looks quickly toward door.*]

HAGAR

Dat's jes' Gilly Bluton's car.

LISSA

[*To* HAGAR.]
Grandma's thirty years behind the times. She never lets me out of her sight. This is the first road house dance I have ever been to and Gardenia had a time of it persuading her to let me go to that.

MAMBA

I ain't likes these free and easy young fellers. One of them kiss Gardenia right in de car. Yo' ain't do t'ing like dat, is you, Lissa?

LISSA

[*Laughing superiorly.*]
You can be mighty sure I'll never let either of these small time Romeos kiss me. [*To* HAGAR.] But no one thinks anything now-a-days of a few kisses.

HAGAR

Dat's de trut'. A few kisses ain't do no harm. [*Very earnestly.*] But, daughtuh, you must always 'member: kissin' got cousin.

MAMBA

[*To* LISSA.]

Tell Maum' Vina good-bye. Yo' mightn't see um when you come out again.

LISSA

[*Putting her arm affectionately over the old woman's shoulder and shouting in her ear.*]

Good-bye, Maum' Vina. I'm going to New York, you know.

VINA

All de way to New Yo'k? [LISSA *nods.*] To live? [LISSA *nods again.* VINA *knocks on the floor with her stick.*] Lissen here, everybody. Hagar' gal goin' to New Yo'k to live. Le's we all give um de good-bye song. [*She starts to sing.*]

> Sistuh Lissa, we goin' leabe yo' in de han',
> We goin' leabe yo' in de han',
> We goin' leabe yo' in de han'
> Ob de kin' Sab-yor.

[*Reluctantly, but taking the hint, the negroes join.* EVA *steps forward to* LISSA *and shakes her hand as she sings. Then leads the way out the door. Slowly they all move toward the door,* HAGAR'S *intimate friends waiting one behind the other to shake* LISSA'S *hand. The others nod their farewells from doorway as they pass out. Then* VINA *again rises from her keg and last of all approaches* LISSA. *Instead of "Sistuh Lissa," she sings:*]

Oh, my daughtuh, now I leabe yo' in de han'
Ob de kin' Sab-yor.

[*Kisses* LISSA *on forehead.* LISSA *drops curtsy.* VINA
*goes last out the door. The voices trail off into the
distance.* MAMBA *and* HAGAR *also take* LISSA's *hand
in farewell and* LISSA *kisses each but says nothing.
Then she follows the others outside. There is the
sound of a starting motor which recedes in the distance. An auto horn sounds faintly.* MAMBA *sinks
into a chair.* HAGAR *leans against the door jamb
looking into the night. Sings softly.*]

HAGAR

Oh, my daughtuh, now I leabe yo' in de han' of de kin'
Sab-yor.

[*The light fades quickly. The stage is dark to indicate
the passing of five hours.*]

[*The door is closed now. In the darkness there is
nothing but the faint glow of* HAGAR's *pipe, her dim
silhouette against the window as she sits smoking in
the big chair. A car stops outside. There is sudden
loud knocking at the door.*]

HAGAR

Who's dat? Who's knockin'?

GARDENIA

[*Outside.*]

It's me, Gardenia. Let me in.

[HAGAR *unlocks and opens the door and* GARDENIA, *panting, comes inside, closes door and leans against it.*]

MAMBA

       [*Raising up from her pallet on the floor.*]
What's de matter?

HAGAR

Whar's Lissa?

GARDENIA

She's gone—   Gone with Prince.

HAGAR

Who's dat?   Prince?—who he?

GARDENIA

Prince—that's all I know.

HAGAR

Whar she gone wid um?

GARDENIA

I think he's taken her to his shack.

HAGAR

Whar dat?

GARDENIA

I don't know.

HAGAR

Jes' Lissa wid dis man?

GARDENIA

Yes.

HAGAR

[*Fiercely.*]

Why you let um go?

GARDENIA

I didn't know.   He gave us some drinks; they must have been knock-out drops.

HAGAR

How long dey been gone?

GARDENIA

I don't know.   I was out cold, an hour maybe.

HAGAR

Why you ain't watch um?

GARDENIA

I passed out cold, I tell you.

HAGAR

You say you goin' to take care ob my gal.

GARDENIA

[*Shrinking away.*]

I meant to—

HAGAR

[Advancing threateningly.]

You say right here you goin' take care ob my gal. *Whar is she?*

MAMBA

[Arrestingly.]

Hagar!

HAGAR

[With immediate submission.]

Yes, Ma?

MAMBA

[To GARDENIA.*]*

Who dis man Prince?

GARDENIA

Prince. That's what everybody calls him in town. That's all the name I know. Oh, Grandma, I meant to look after her like I promised you but I passed out cold. I went to lie down and when I came back, Lissa was gone.

MAMBA

Lissa been drinkin'?

GARDENIA

Yes, she must have been drunk, too, or she'd never have gone with him.

MAMBA

We got to find 'em quick.   Who'd know where dis Prince
live?

GARDENIA

I've been to his shack.   It's way in the marsh.   I wouldn't
know how to find it by myself.

HAGAR

On Ediwander?   But I know everybody on Ediwander.
Ain't nobody name Prince.

GARDENIA

He was right here this evening.

HAGAR

Here in the store?

GARDENIA

Yes.   He was all the time sitting back there on the
counter.

HAGAR

You ain't mean—Gilly Bluton?

GARDENIA

That's right.   Somebody called him Gilly.

HAGAR

[*Dazed.*]

But—Gilly Bluton—he was good as daid.   I gib um back
he life.

MAMBA

Shut up. We got to find um. You know where he live?

HAGAR

It's straight across the marsh. I goin' fo' um.
[*Runs to door.*]

MAMBA

Wait fo' me, gal.

HAGAR

You can't go, Ma. I goin' straight t'rough the marsh.
It's a long way 'roun' by the road.

MAMBA

[*Seizing her.*]

I goin' wid yo'.

HAGAR

[*Violently shaking her off.*]
No, Ma, yo'd hol' me back.
[HAGAR *runs out with* MAMBA *still protesting.*
MAMBA *starts after her.*]

GARDENIA

[*Holding her.*]
Grandma! Listen!

MAMBA

I gots to go to my baby.

GARDENIA

You can't keep up with Hagar. You'd get lost in the marsh.

MAMBA

Lemme go.

GARDENIA

It's pitch dark and it's beginning to rain.

MAMBA

[*Calling.*]

Hagar, wait fo' me.

GARDENIA

You wait here with me. Hagar'll bring um.

MAMBA

I got to go. I can't trus' dat daughtuh ob mine. Yo' go on home, Gardenia. Yo' done what you could. *Hagar!* I'm comin'.

[*Shakes* GARDENIA *off.   Runs out.*]

[*Quick black-out.   Into the darkness the music from a cheap radio crashes suddenly, blaring out a popular dance tune such as "Boo Hoo."*]

ACT THREE

SCENE 2: GILLY's *cabin. It is lighted dimly by a lamp on crap table which stands a little back of center. Entrance to cabin is through adjoining room. The door of this room is in left wall near the front. There are windows at back and between them are hung some hunting paraphernalia, guns and a knife. There is little furniture except for the table and a number of chairs, but what there is is less rickety than that of a typical negro cabin. There is a radio against right wall. Its dial is lighted and the music heard between the scenes is issuing from it.*

LISSA *is sitting on the floor at right, her back to audience, her head leant sideways against the wall.* GILLY *is standing near her.*

GILLY

Come on now, Baby. Enough's enough.

[*Leans down to pick her up.*]

LISSA

Don't touch me.

GILLY

Aw, cut it out. You put on a damned good show but I had plenty. [*Radio rasps with static. He turns it down.*] Come on, Baby. Be sensible. If you want me to, I'll take you home now.

LISSA

Why didn't I kill you?

GILLY

[*Growing impatient.*]

Oh, cut the bunk!   You make me sick.   [*Again whee-dling.*]   Listen, honey.   You and me ain't through.   Not by a long shot.   Why, Baby, I'm crazy 'bout you.

[*Turns up radio.   Tries several stations.   Finds music he likes.*]

LISSA

[*Looking at knife on wall.*]

I had the chance.   You weren't looking.   There was that knife.

GILLY

Shut up, Baby.   I had about enough.   What you need is a little pick-up.   Hair of the dog's the thing.   Just a minute.

[*He goes into adjoining room where he makes a light. The light from this brightly lighted room throws a path across the dimly lighted room on stage. As* GILLY *returns with whiskey for* LISSA, *his shadow comes before him.*]

GILLY

[*Offering drink.*]

Try this, Baby.   [LISSA *draws farther from him.*]   Come on.   It will pick you up.   [LISSA *pays no attention.   He drinks it himself.   The radio gives more static and he turns it off.*] We better be going on our way soon. Tide's coming in. Flood tide tonight and it's raining hard. Might be we couldn't get across the causeway an hour from now.

[*Stands near* LISSA, *looking down at her, cajoling her. As he talks a shadow crosses the floor and grows huge against the wall, a little to the back of spot where* LISSA *crouches, then is motionless.*]

GILLY

Oh, for God's sake, stop the sniveling and get up off the floor. I'll drive you back to Charleston whenever you say, but don't you forget it—you're coming back. Never knew a girl yet who wasn't all ready to come again. But there aren't going to be any others from now on. Just you and me, Baby.

[*He raises his eyes and sees the shadow. For an instant he stares at it fascinated. Then he swings around and faces door. He draws in his breath in an audible gasp but does not speak.* HAGAR *comes into room. She sees* LISSA *and goes to her.* GILLY *backs away from them to left.*]

HAGAR

Baby, is yo' hurt?

LISSA

No.

HAGAR

Yo' shore yo' is all right?

LISSA

Yes.   Don't touch me.

HAGAR

[*Gently.*]

Lissa, I goin' take yo' home.

LISSA

Go away.   Let me be.
   [*Begins to sob hysterically. HAGAR swings around suddenly and faces GILLY. In her distressed, childlike
   face there grows slowly an expression of such savage
   hate and rage that GILLY's jaw drops and he shrinks
   back against wall at left, his knees all but giving
   under him.*]

HAGAR

[*Slowly.*]

Yo' was daid.   I gave yo' back yo' life.   Fo' dis.   Fo'
hurt my baby.
   [*She moves slowly, inexorably toward him.*]

GILLY

[*With unconvincing bravado.*]

Now don't try to start anything, Sister.   Lissa's got a
right to come here if she wants to.   Get on out of here.   Go
home where you belong.
   [*As she approaches, he slides along the wall toward the
   door. LISSA is crouching against the wall, her breath
   coming in quick gasps punctuated by a sob of terror.*]

[*GILLY makes a sudden dash for the door. Then instantly HAGAR is upon him. Has him around the throat. He beats wildly at her and pushes her back from him until they have struggled together to center of room. HAGAR's back to the audience, her great shoulders arched by the power of her grip. GILLY's arms cease to annoy her. They feebly beat the air. From outside MAMBA's voice shrieks in wild horror.*]

MAMBA

Hagar! Drap um. [*HAGAR's shoulders relax suddenly. He slips from her grip. Falls on his knees. MAMBA staggers in. Her clothes are torn and wet to the waist. Her gray hair streams. Her face is distorted by fear.*] Oh, Gawd! Gawd hab' mercy.

[*She staggers to chair at right front and sinks onto it. She is shaking with exhaustion and dread. GILLY struggles to his feet, lunges to the door and out.*]

MAMBA

[*Reverently.*]

I t'ank yo', Gawd, fo' let me get here in time. [*Then she looks at HAGAR who, her back still to audience, has wilted completely, her shoulders sagging, her head hanging down like a child caught in disobedience. MAMBA's face hardens.*] You fool. You Gawd-damned big blunderin' fool. What de hell did yo' t'ink yo' was doin'? Oh, Gawd, why you gots to saddle me wid dis? Can't I lef' um one minute widout she do some fool t'ing?

HAGAR

[Defensively.]

He hurt Lissa.

MAMBA

[Glancing sadly but briefly at the cowering LISSA.*]*

I'm mighty sorry 'bout dat but *yo'* is the one that's tryin' to hurt um so nothin' can ever make um right again.

HAGAR

Me? Hurt Lissa, Ma?

MAMBA

If I come one minute later, dat man daid, ain't he? *[*MAMBA *is so exhausted, she has to stop for breath between each sentence.]* How yo' t'ink dat goin' to be for Lissa? How many people yo' t'ink saw Lissa leabe dat dance hall wid dat yaller son of a bitch. Eberybody see um. They goin' put in all de papers how Lissa been wid um an' den how he foun' daid in his cabin. De cops get yo' an' dey make yo' talk. Yo' know dey can make yo' talk. Dey can even make smart people talk; an' dey goin' ax yo' why yo' done um. An' dey goin' keep on axin' yo' till yo' tells um. Den dey goin' to put in de paper how Lissa's ma— what got jail sentence befo'—been set in de 'lectric chair fo' killin' dat dirty nigger. An' why?—'Cause he been sleepin' wid Lissa. Dat goin' be fine fo' Lissa, ain't it? Wid a ma like yo', what chance dat gal got?

HAGAR

> [*Sobbing with fear at the picture* MAMBA *paints.*]
> I ain't hurt um, Ma.   He got away, enty?   He all right.
> [MAMBA *turns and looks at* LISSA *and is suddenly all
> tenderness.*]

MAMBA

> My poor little baby.   Come here to yo' old grandma.
> [LISSA *shakes her head and does not move.   Anxiously.*]
> Yo' ain't hurt, is yo'?

LISSA

> No.

HAGAR

> [*Going to her.*]
> Can't you get up, Lissa?

LISSA

> Please let me alone.

HAGAR

> Yo' grandma an' me goin' take yo' home now.
> [LISSA *does not answer.*]

MAMBA

> I can't go jus' yet.   I done in.   Mebbe yo' better take
Lissa along if you think that Bluton nigger might come back
here.

HAGAR

He ain't comin' back here.   Not dis night.   [*Looks from window.*]   Rainin' hard out an' a pitch black night.   We bes' wait awhile.

MAMBA

Can't be very long now till firs' light.   [*Gets up and goes to* LISSA.]   Yo' mustn't carry on so, gal.   Eberyt'ing goin' be all right.   [LISSA *does not answer.   She turns her face from her grandma.*]   Lissen, honey chile, dese t'ings happen. Dey happen to lots of the gals yo' know, an' many of dose ain't got de decency to feel bery bad about um.   It's goin' to be all right, honey.   [LISSA *catches her breath in a sob and turns her face to the wall.*]   I guess yo' t'ink I'm mighty hard talkin' dis way so soon but yo' gots to see t'ing as dey is. It's jus' somet'in' to forget.   If yo' should have a baby your ma an' me'd take care of it jes' like we done yo'.   It'll take a yeah out of your life, dat's de trut'.   But after dat yo' could go to Noo Yo'k jus' de same.   An' if you don' hab no baby, why, den, eberyt'ing is jus' like it was.   Only your ma an' me an' Gardenia know.

LISSA

He knows and I know.

MAMBA

Poor little lamb.   Don't think yo' ole grandma's heart-strings ain't rip apart fo' yo'.   But it jus' fo' a little while, daughtuh, an' den eberyt'ing'll be all right again.

LISSA

You're a fine one to tell me that.

MAMBA

I knows, darlin'. I tries to bring yo' up to t'ink dat to hab t'ings like this happen to yo' was the end ob eberyt'ing. I do dat, Lissa, 'cause I neber want any unhappiness like dis to come near yo'. But it come; an' I tells yo' de trut' now. Yo' still got de same life, de same pretty face an' same pretty voice. An' mighty soon now yo' goin' be in Noo Yo'k studyin' an' learnin' an' singin'—an' forgettin'.

LISSA

I won't be forgetting, not ever. So long as that man lives I'll feel ashamed, hate myself. I'm different from you. You talk about forgetting. I'll never forget so long as he remembers. I could have killed him. I wish I had.

MAMBA

Lissen, chile—

LISSA

[*Leaping to her feet.*]

There's no use in my listening. I know what you'll say. But I'm different, I tell you. You did it. You made me different. Since I was old enough to talk you've been pre- paring me for a thing like this—so that it would kill me inside.

MAMBA

There's no use talkin' now when yo' upset, chile. Come here to yo' ole grandma and put down yo' haid an' res' awhile.

LISSA

I'm so tired. Let me alone.
          [*Sinks down in corner at right back.*]

MAMBA

Dat's right. We'll all get a little res'. Den soon firs' daylight we'll start fo' home. I'll lay me down over here. Help me down, Daughtuh. [HAGAR *eases her down on the floor at back of room. Finds a cushion for her.*] T'ank yo'. Yo' mus' be mighty weary yo'self. Stretch out an' get some res'. Jus' lissen to dat rain. Nobody comin' here in dat. [HAGAR *sits against wall at right front, leans back and stretches out her legs.*] If I been too hard on yo', Daughtuh, I sorry. Guess I said more'n I meant count of bein' so scared 'bout Lissa. [*Drowsily.*] Dat right, yo' stretch out an' get some res'—an' jus' try to 'membuh not to go ahead an' do t'ings—till yo' ax me whedder or not it's bes' to do um.

          [MAMBA *is almost instantly asleep.* HAGAR *lies still.
          After a moment* LISSA *rises up, looks at them, gets
          quietly to her feet, creeps cautiously to door.*]

HAGAR

Where yo' goin', Lissa?

LISSA

I was just going out—in the air. I can't stand it to stay here tonight.

HAGAR

Goin' be gettin' light very soon now.

LISSA

I can't stand it here.

HAGAR

Yo' grandma right in all she say to you. Yo' don' believe she, do you?

LISSA

You and she don't understand. [*Going over to her.*] Don't you think I know how things have been with you and with grandma? I know I've got no father and I never heard talk of a grandfather either. I'm not holding anything against you, Mother, or against grandmother. What you've done is all right for you. But you and grandma can't understand—me. [*Crouches on her knees, facing* HAGAR *with mounting hysteria.*] I'm not like that. She says it doesn't really matter. It matters to me. I'm dif—

HAGAR

[*Quietly.*]
Course yo's different, Lissa. Yo' mudder un'erstan'. [LISSA *has not expected this. She breaks off in her tirade*

and stares at her mother.]   I ain't ever t'ink yo' like me an'
Mamba.   No, yo' is different, Lissa.   But when a t'ing is
done an' nothing can make um undone, yo' gots to jus' go
on livin'.   My little gal.   Yo' so weary.   Yo' can hardly
set up.   Res' a little bit.   Put yo' head in my lap.   So weary,
chile.

LISSA

[*Getting to her feet.*]
I can't stay here.   Let me go.

HAGAR

Full tide now.   I can hear um lappin' at the piles.   An'
lissen how de rain fallin'.   It pitch black now in de marsh—
an' so wet.   I could hardly fin' de way myself now.   [LISSA
hesitates, returns to her.]   It's de dark befo' de firs' dawn.
Jus' a little while—an' my gal so weary.   [LISSA *sinks down
beside her.*]   Put yo' head down an' res'.

LISSA

I'm so tired.   [LISSA *lies with her head in* HAGAR'S *lap.
Pause.*]   Mother.

HAGAR

Hush, my baby.   Try to res'.   [*Complete quiet for a moment.*   HAGAR *goes to stroke* LISSA'S *hair, but is afraid she
may resent it.*]   Dey t'ink I got a funny way settin' alone
in de evenin's singin' to myself an' all de time I been singin'
my baby to sleep.   It been like dis many nights with yo'
head in my lap.

LISSA

[*Whispering.*]

Mother.

HAGAR

No, yo' ain't really been there. [LISSA *lies quiet. After a moment* HAGAR *begins softly to hum. She sings in a low, soft voice.*]

Do, my Lor',
Do, my Lor'.
Ain't 'e rain—

LISSA

Mother. [HAGAR *quiet.*] I didn't know.

HAGAR

What yo' didn't know?

LISSA

I didn't know—you. I mean—I never stopped to think about the money. How hard you worked. Mr. Saint, he knew. He said— Sometimes she'd urge me to go with her to see you—Grandma, I mean—urge me a little. But Saturday was always choir practice, and there were parties—and I always thought I'd go the next time. It was always to be the next time, Mother—I just didn't think. I never really knew you.

HAGAR

Dat's all right, Lissa. I never wanted you to miss any fun. Try to res', honey.

[*Hums.* LISSA *raises her head.*]

LISSA

Mother—tell me—I've always wanted to know. [HAGAR
waits.] My— That song you sang in the store this evening— You said, "You know my man—"

HAGAR

It's jus' a song, honey. Don't mean nuttin'. Jus' a song.
[*Hesitantly.*] Yo' grandma ain't give me de bringin'-up
she give you. I so big for my age—seems like I can't remember when dere wasn't men. An' some of 'em was bright-
skinned and some is dark. But neber any white man. Ef
dat's what yo' been thinkin'. Baby, put yo' mind at res'.
Dey comes an' dey goes—an' dat's huccum I ain't quite
sure— My little gal, don't think too hard on yo' ma. Since
first I holds you, dere's been no men at all. Nobody 'cep'
you. Nobody in all dis worl' 'cep' only you.

[LISSA *sinks back with head in* HAGAR's *lap.*]

LISSA

I'm going to make it all up to you now. I'm going to
work so hard. Just the two times I sang here in Charleston,
the radio people said I was good. They said I had a future.
I'm going to make money, lots of it. Then you can stop
working and you and Grandma can live together in Charleston. I'll buy you a big radio so that whenever I sing over
the radio you must listen to me. I know I can do it. I—
[*Gasps.*] I'll never sing again.

[*Buries her face in* HAGAR's *lap, sobbing.*]

HAGAR

We cullud people got one t'ing over de white folks. Dere ain't no trouble so big that we can't sing about um. Bes' t'ing fo' trouble is singin'—an' workin'. And when yo' work is singin' den yo' is holdin' a charm 'gainst trouble.

[*Hums.*]

LISSA

Mother. [HAGAR *hums more softly.*] Sometimes I could hardly remember what you looked like. But I always thought of you singing. I remember all the songs you used to sing to me. When I was about ten or twelve I used to come oftener, didn't I?

HAGAR

Dose were de days.

LISSA

I didn't think—

HAGAR

De work never seem hard. I had what I wanted. Since de day yo' was born I ain't wanted nothin' 'cept that you grow up good and beautiful—like yo' is—an' happy like you goin' to be soon as I can fix it. Don't yo' worry none, my baby. Yo' ma always goin' take care of yo'. [*Hums a moment. Then sings.*]

CURTAIN

ACT FOUR

ACT FOUR

SCENE 1: *The store, at the present time. It is the same night and same hour as Prologue. Practically the only change in store is the addition of a small radio on a stand against left wall.* SAINT *is alone at his desk. In the church a spiritual is being sung:*

> I goin' 'cross dat separatin' line
> An' I'll leabe dis worl' behin'.

HAGAR *comes in. She has changed more in the last three years than in all the years preceding. Again her dress is old and faded.*
SAINT *looks up.*

SAINT
Why, Hagar! Not at church?

HAGAR
No, Mr. Saint. Lissa's singin' tonight. Yo' ain't hear'? Dis is de night she hab her big openin' ober de radio.

SAINT
Oh, is this the night? Well, I meant to hear that myself. Maybe I'll get to Charleston in time for the last part of it. You want to hear it over my radio?

HAGAR

Yes, if you please, suh.

SAINT

Is it time?

HAGAR

It begins at nine o'clock.

SAINT

[Looking at watch.]
In twelve—thirteen minutes. *[Leans back in his chair, looking up at her.]* Well, this is the big night, isn't it, Hagar? The night you planned and worked for all these years.

HAGAR

[Happily.]
Dat's de trut', Mr. Saint.

SAINT

Your daughter's a star now. Isn't it about time for you to stop working so hard and go back to town to live with Mamba?

HAGAR

[Uneasily.]
I been a country nigger so long I done forget city way'. An' I likes to keep workin'. Ef I ain't workin' when all de odder nigger is, I got too much time on my hand'—too much

time fo' t'inkin'. [*Laughing a little.*] It's like Mamba's allus tellin' me. De good Gawd ain't mean me fo' t'ink.

SAINT

Tell me the truth, Hagar. After the way you and Mamba slaved for her, doesn't that girl of yours send you any money?

HAGAR

[*Bridling.*]

Dere neber was a gal do better by she ma an' gran'ma. Dat gal can't sen' 'nuff. Jus' mont' befo' las' she sen' ma one t'ousand dollah.

SAINT

Hagar, you and I have always been friends. I know what you buy. You are living on less than any hand on the plantation, doing the work of two men. Why don't you tell me the truth?

HAGAR

It's the Gawd's trut', Mr. Saint. [*Seeing* SAINT's *skeptical look she reaches in bosom of her dress and takes out envelope.*] Here, dis letter come five day' ago. Dis what she sen' me. [*Takes folded bills from envelope. Hands them to* SAINT.] Count um.

SAINT

[*Counts.*]

Ten ten dollar bills, one hundred dollars. Well, for God's sake, Hagar, buy yourself some food and some new clothes.   You used to be always admiring the new dresses in this store when you couldn't afford them.   Now you can afford them and you are almost in rags.   [HAGAR *says nothing.   Looks miserable.*]   Well?

[HAGAR *seems to be thinking deeply.   Again takes envelope from front of dress.*]

HAGAR

Mr. Saint, I in bery great trouble.
[*She looks irresolutely at the envelope.*]

SAINT

Bad news?

HAGAR

I don't know.   I ain't read um.

SAINT

Do you want me to read it to you?

HAGAR

Please, Mr. Saint.   [*Hands it to him.*]   Lissa know I can't read so she allus sen' letter' to Ma so as Gardenia can read um fo' we.   But dis letter come here an' she say it ain't for Ma, it jes' fo' me an' I don't know what it say.

SAINT

You've had it five days?

HAGAR

I ax Willie May to read um fo' me, but— [*Nods toward letter.*] You'll see.

SAINT

[*Reads.*]

"Dearest Mother: Get someone you can trust to read this letter to you. It's just for you. Not for Grandma—"

HAGAR

Willie May read dat. I say to um, "Mus' be dis letter's somet'in' very special" and I take um away f'om um.

SAINT

You trust me, don't you, Hagar?

HAGAR

You, Mr. Saint? Sho' I trus' you.

SAINT

[*Reads.*]

"Mother, dear, after the way you and Grandma have worked for me, it would break my heart to have you think me ungrateful. It's been the dream of my life to give you everything you could want. But how can you want so much? In the last four months I have sent—"

[HAGAR *covers letter with her hand.*]

HAGAR
Better not read um, Mr. Saint.

SAINT
[*Gives her a long, level look.*]
Who is to read it, Hagar?
[HAGAR *silently withdraws hand.*]

SAINT
[*Reads.*]
"I have sent Grandma three thousand dollars. I thought
you would consider that a fortune, but every letter asks for
more. There must be something Grandma is not telling me.
I am wondering if she has made up her mind to collect all
my money and put it up for my old age. If so, she is wrong.
They are trying to put me across as a big star and that costs
money. They want me to be seen in gorgeous clothes and
live in a fine apartment. Mother, dear, try to persuade
Grandma to live on what you have for a few months. Then
I can send more. Don't forget to be listening to me next
Wednesday night. I am putting in some spending money
just for you. Your devoted daughter, Lissa."

[SAINT *silently folds the letter and hands it back to*
HAGAR. *Seeing him look questioningly at her she
unfolds it and stares miserably at the writing as
though pretending to read it.*]

SAINT
You don't want to tell me anything?   [HAGAR *dumbly
shakes head. Returns letter to bosom. Presses it to her with
both hands.*]   Is Mamba hoarding the money?

HAGAR

[*Too glibly.*]

Yes, suh. She 'fraid Lissa spend um all. She want to put um in de bank fo' she.

SAINT

Why do you say you trust me?

HAGAR

Mr. Saint—I'd lay my soul in yo' han' fo' safe keepin' but Lissa—she all I got.

SAINT

[*Giving it up.*]

I'd like to help. Well, I'll turn on the radio for you. [*Starts toward his room. Then looks back at her and seeing her wretchedness makes one more try.*] What do you do with the money, Hagar?

HAGAR

[*Draws in her breath in a hopeless sigh.*]

I gib um to Gilly Bluton.

SAINT

[*Astonished.*]

Gilly Bluton? [HAGAR *nods.*] Why?

HAGAR

To keep his Gawd-damned mout' from openin'.

SAINT

[*Returning to her.*]

He's been blackmailing you?   You've been paying him not to tell something?

HAGAR

Yes.

SAINT

What?

HAGAR

'Bout Lissa's baby.

SAINT

Lissa had a baby?

HAGAR

Yes, suh.

SAINT

Where is it?

HAGAR

[*Desperately.*]

Mr. Saint, I tells yo' de Gawd's trut'.   I'd have given my life fo' save dat baby.   Ma, too.   Ma know' eberyt'ing 'bout catchin' baby.   Ain't nobody know better what to do.   We do eberyt'ing—eberyt'ing.   It ain't die 'cause eberyt'ing ain't done fo' um, it die 'cause Lissa grieb' an' fret an' she won' eat an' w'en dat baby born he was so little an' puny, he only lib an hour. But Ma an' me did ebery Gawd's t'ing to save um. I swears dat to yo'.

SAINT

Gilly Bluton was the father?

HAGAR

[*Nodding her head.*]
My Lissa's a good gal. But one night she gone to a dance and Gilly Bluton got um drunk. Dat was easy 'cause she'd neber tasted licker befo' an' den—

SAINT

And you've been paying him to keep his mouth shut?

HAGAR

[*Nods.*]
He say it bery strange 'bout huccum de baby to die an' eberyt'ing so secret. He say de police goin' want to know 'bout huccum dat baby die.

SAINT

How long has this been going on?

HAGAR

He began comin' 'roun' jus' as soon as she get her big job singin' on de radio. He say, "Get me a t'ousand dollah from Lissa an' I won't say nothin' to nobody." An' we give um to um. An' pretty soon he come back an' he say, "Get um another t'ousand." Each time we t'ink he ain't goin' come no more. He say he ain't comin' no more but he always come back.

SAINT

Hagar, good God. Why didn't you come to me before! How many of your friends out here have doctors when their babies are born? They have midwives and if Mamba's been acting as a midwife—why, Gilly Bluton would have had better sense than to have even made the charge. He was just taking you for a ride.

HAGAR

You mean, Mr. Saint, I ain't had to pay um all dat money?

SAINT

Certainly *not*. At least— Suppose you tell me just what happened.

HAGAR

Well, suh, you see jus' after—jus' after Gilly—

SAINT

Yes, I understand.

HAGAR

We sen' Lissa to Noo Yo'k and she gettin' on fine up there an' her teacher write an' say she goin' be fine singer. Den Lissa fin' out she goin' hab de baby, an' she ain't want people in Noo Yo'k to know. So we bring um back to

Cha'leston an' she hide in Mamba' room till de time come. Den Ma, she bring um down here an' Maum' Vina take she in. De baby come in Vina' cabin. Ma was goin' to take it an' raise it. But it ain't live so we bury it in de woods an' ain't say nuttin'.

SAINT

Great God, do you mean you never reported the birth to the authorities?

HAGAR

We ain't know dat matter so much an' eberybody would have know' 'bout Lissa.

SAINT

Didn't you know you could be tried for murder for that?

HAGAR

Dat what Gilly say—an' he say he goin' hab us fryin' in de chair if we ain't come 'cross.

SAINT

What evidence has he got?

HAGAR

He git wind of it somehow after Lissa was back in New York. An' he devil poor ole Vina till she git weak in de head an' break down an' tell him. Den he make a writin' an' she put her mark on it.

[*A pause.* HAGAR *looks anxiously at* SAINT.]

SAINT
[*Slowly.*]

Well, there's no use trying to fool you.   He's got you on the spot.   [*Looks at his watch.*]   Why, hello!   It's past time.   We're missing the great moment.   [*Switches on radio.*]

> RADIO.—LISSA's *voice is heard finishing "That Hallelu-jah Song."   Applause at end of song.*

That's one of your songs, Hagar.

HAGAR
[*Proudly.*]

Lissa say dey writes dis show special for her an' dey put in some of de songs she an' me used to sing togedder w'en she was a little gal.

SAINT

Just listen to that applause, Hagar.

> RADIO.—LISSA *begins to speak.*

SAINT
[*Looking through door and beginning simultaneously with* LISSA.]

I see church is out, and here comes your daughter's public. I'll tell them they'll have to keep quiet if they come in here so that you—

HAGAR

Wait, Mr. Saint.   Dat's Lissa talkin', ain't it?
[SAINT *breaks off.   Stands listening.*]

RADIO.—LISSA: —way down South she is listening to
me tonight. And on this, the biggest night of my
life, I want her to hear me say, "Mother, I owe this
all—to you."

[*An expression of unbelieving amazement comes into*
HAGAR's *face, then changes to exultation.*]

RADIO.—*Applause. Orchestra plays softly.*

HAGAR

[*The ecstasy suddenly fading into uncertainty.*]
Dat's somet'ing in de play, ain't it?

SAINT

She said that straight to you.
    [HAGAR *rises slowly, goes to radio.*]

HAGAR

T'ank yo', Lissa. Dat mighty sweet of yo', Baby.

RADIO.—*The orchestra starts the prelude to the song,
playing softly. Announcer repeats introductory com-
ments made in Prologue.*

[*In twos and threes the negroes enter store and crowd
around the radio. Intent on getting good places, they
elbow* HAGAR *out of the way, until she is withdrawn
from the group and stands looking uncertainly toward them.*]

SAINT

    [*Laying a hand on* HAGAR's *shoulder.*]
Don't worry over Gilly too much. There must be some
way to stop his mouth. We'll have to think hard.

HAGAR

Yes, we'll hab to t'ink hard.

SAINT

[*To* DAVEY, *who has entered last of the negroes.*]
Lock up when the concert's over.
[*Goes.*]
RADIO.—*The orchestra pauses for a beat and* LISSA's
voice comes through clearly in the first verse of
"*Lonesome Walls.*"

A WOMAN

Dat's Hagar's gal now!

A MAN

Hot dog!   Dat's some singin'.

A WOMAN

Bet she cain't sing dis like Hagar!
[*But the crowd has forgotten* HAGAR. *Close about the
radio, their arms across each other's shoulders, they
sway to the music in rapt enjoyment.* HAGAR *stands
alone at some distance; her lips move in a tremendous
effort at concentration. She hoists her skirt and from
a pocket in petticoat takes out some crumpled bills.
She smooths them out and counts them; then she
takes the letter from her bosom, removes bills, re-
places letter, and rolls these bills up with the others
in her hand. Slowly, still in deep thought, she moves
toward the door and out into the night. And, as she*

goes, LISSA'S *voice finishes the first verse, and the lights fade.]*

[In the darkness the orchestra plays an interlude between verses of "Dem Lonesome Walls." A radio dial—on opposite side of stage from that of Scene 1 —lights up. LISSA'S *voice begins second verse.]*

ACT FOUR

SCENE 2: *As the light increases a solitary shadowy figure is not exactly dancing but moving in rhythm to the music. The full light, never very bright, reveals* GILLY's *cabin. As in Act Three, Scene 2, a single lamp is on the table and a path of light streams from the more brightly lighted adjoining room.*

The dancing figure is GILLY, *who is in an ecstasy of remembrance. Hoofing to* LISSA's *music, always facing radio, dancing toward it, then backing away in grotesque but not ungraceful rhythm.*

GILLY

Come on, Baby! [HAGAR's *shadow appears on wall, not directly in* GILLY's *line of vision. It advances slowly until it is of huge proportions, then is motionless.*] Sing, Baby, sing!

[*A half turn brings him up facing shadow. He springs behind the crap table, takes a revolver from table-drawer. As soon as he has the revolver he is completely reassured. He lays it on the table before him. Then he stands watching the door, by which she will enter, with casual indifference.* HAGAR *advances slowly into the room. Her dress is wet and muddy from crossing the marsh. She takes up her position on the other side of the table facing* GILLY.]

160

GILLY

Well, Big Gal!   I ain't been expecting you till after de show but I can take it any time.

> RADIO.—LISSA's *voice finishes second verse.   Orchestra plays interlude.*
>
> [NOTE: *At this point radio conveniently fades so that dialogue can be distinctly heard above it.   Or the whole orchestral interlude could be played in lower key.*]

You got it?

HAGAR

I ain't got all you say but I bring what I got.
> [*She lays a small roll of bills on the table.*]

GILLY

Open it out an' throw 'em down one at a time so's I can count 'em.   [HAGAR *picks up roll and obeys.*]   One hundred and nine dollars.   I tol' you two hundred dis week.

HAGAR

She ain't sen' me but de hundred.   De nine's my own wages.

GILLY

You ever tell her you is puttin' in yo' own money?

HAGAR

No.   I ain't tell um nuttin'.

GILLY

If you was to tell her dat I bet she'd come across herself. [*He pauses and a look of suspicion comes into his face.*] Look here. She knows who gets this, doesn't she? You told her you were giving it to me and why, didn't you?

HAGAR

[*Doggedly.*]

We ain't tell um nuttin'.

GILLY

Well, what do you tell her?

HAGAR

We jus' tell um we needs it. Dat Ma sick an' got to pay de doctor. Dat I needs new clo'es—

GILLY

[*Getting excited.*]

Great God! You mean to say I ain't gettin' nuttin' but de chicken feed she sends you two niggers?

HAGAR

[*Frightened.*]

What you care how we gets it. We brings it to yo', ain't it? [*She senses the triumph in his voice and manner.*] An' nex' week I'll bring more—two hundred, maybe.

GILLY

You needn't worry yo'self about that. You ain't going to have to bring me any more at all.

HAGAR

What yo' means?

GILLY

I means I'm through cashin' in on a two bits lottery ticket. I'm goin' to collect de gran' prize. I'm movin' to headquarters, Big Gal.

HAGAR

Headquarters?

GILLY

You think I like dis dump! Peddlin' licker to you niggers, shakin' you down for lousy little dimes an' nickels on dis table. Lickin' de police boots, so's I can make an' hones' livin'. I always knew that someday I'd go to Harlem, cut in on the big money an' now I'm goin'.

HAGAR

What yo' mean, goin'—you ain't goin' to Noo Yo'k?

GILLY

Sure I'm goin' to New Yo'k. If dat gal love you so much that she can sen' you all that jus' fo' spendin' money, there'll be pretty fat pickings when she hears how someday her ma an' gran'ma might be fryin' in the electric chair.

HAGAR

Let me git dis straight in my head. Yo' was daid once. Dey say at de hospital five mo' minute' an' yo' ain't got a

chance.   Nuttin' 'tween yo' an' Almighty Gawd 'cep' five
minute'—an' me.   I gib yo' back yo' life an' now yo' goin'
to do dat to my Lissa.

[*He sees murder in her eye and is instantly on the
    alert.*]

RADIO.—LISSA's *voice begins third verse.*

[*Radio stronger.*]

GILLY

You knows all de answers, Big Gal.

[*She comes slowly around the table toward him.   He
    lets her come near to him then with insolent non-
    chalance picks up the gun.   But he has miscalculated
    her strength and swiftness.   Her attack is so sudden
    that before he can point gun she has wrenched his
    hand over his head, bent it back.   The revolver falls
    to floor.   He leaps to retrieve it but before he can get
    it she kicks it under table out of his reach.   GILLY
    springs upon her, tries to pinion her arms.   They
    struggle.   Then HAGAR flings him back to right and
    herself staggers back against left wall.   After one
    second to catch her breath she starts for him.   GILLY
    seizes the lamp and hurls it at her.   HAGAR dodges.
    Lamp crashes out against wall.   The room is in dark-
    ness except for the path of light from the door and
    the radio dial.   GILLY makes one dash into the path
    of light.   He meets her there.   Her hands close
    around his throat and their figures sway together into
    the surrounding blackness.*]

Above LISSA'S *singing is heard a brief, dreadful gasping for breath.*

Path of light blacks out.

LISSA *finishes third verse. The radio dial goes dark. In the darkness full chorus joins* LISSA *in reprise of third verse.*]

ACT FOUR

SCENE 3: *The lights come on, revealing the store. A number of the negroes are grouped about the radio. Others sit about on kegs and boxes. They are all quiet, listening to the music.* DAVEY *sits back of counter, looking sleepy.*

RADIO.—*The chorus brings "Dem Lonesome Walls" to its conclusion. Announcer:* You have been listening to the all-negro review, "America Sings," starring Lissa Wentworth, brought to you by Sultana Cigarettes. This program has come to you direct from the Forty-second Street Theatre, New York, through the facilities of the Colonial Broadcasting Company. This is Don Arnold saying good night. *Radio chimes sound the hour.*

DAVEY

Turn um off, Mingo. Dat's all dey is.

RADIO.—*Second Announcer:* Station WWSC atop the Francis Marion Hotel down in Charleston, Sou—

[MINGO *switches off radio. The negroes show no signs of leaving.* DAVEY *begins moving among boxes and barrels and forcibly dislodging customers from their perches.*]

DAVEY

All right, you done heard Hagar's gal. Get on home. It's way after closing time. [*Dislodging another customer.*] Git goin'. What yo' t'ink dis is? A boahdin' house? [*Calling.*] Hang up de outside shutters, Ben, den come an' give me a han' wid dese no 'count niggers.

[EVA *and* WILLIE MAY *are moving toward door commenting on play,* VINA *is dozing over her pipe, when* HAGAR *appears in doorway. Her dress is dishevelled but her face is calm. In one hand she carries a revolver and in the other, a folded paper. While the negroes are silent and stare at her, she advances to the counter and lays the revolver down on it. All stare at it, fascinated into silence.* HAGAR *turns her back to the counter, rests her elbows on it and stands looking out over the heads of the negroes in calm detachment. They wait, spellbound.*]

HAGAR

Yo' peoples ever see dat gun befo'?

NEGROES

Yes—dat's Bluton's— Sho' dat's Gilly's.

HAGAR

Has any of yo' eber hear of a nigger killin' he own self by what de white folks calls committin' suicide?

[*For a moment there is awed silence.*]

DAVEY

What you mean?

EVA

Fo' Gawd's sake, Hagar.   Gilly ain't kill he'self?

HAGAR

No, he ain't kill he'self.   I jus' t'inkin'.

DRAYTON

Everybody know nigger never kill he'self.

HAGAR

[*Impersonally.*]

Why dat is?

MINGO

'Cause nigger ain't worry he'self dat much.

HAGAR

[*As though thinking aloud.*]
Ain't allus goin' to be like dat.   Time comin' when nigger goin' worry he'self jus' like white folks.   An' then when he trouble get too deep fo' um to wade through all alone, Gawd goin' show um what to do.

[*She continues to stand there.   Pause.*]

DAVEY

Closin' time, Sister.

HAGAR

Don't close um yet, son.   I got some business to attend to 'fore I go.   [*Extends paper for* DAVEY *to see.   With one hand she covers it so that he can see only the signature.*] Who name is dat, Davey?

DAVEY

Dat Vina Dawson mark.

HAGAR

I thought so.   [*She picks up match box from counter, strikes match, lights paper, holding it by one corner and watching it until it burns out.   Then she turns and deliberately looks merchandise over.   Points to large jar of candy balls.*]   How much dat bottle of jawbreakers?

DAVEY

[*Amazed.*]

De whole t'ing?

HAGAR

Shore, de whole t'ing.

DAVEY

Well, there mus' be mo' than a hunderd in dere.   Dat be one dollah an' twenty cent'.

[*With a broad gesture,* HAGAR *lifts jar, withdraws stopper, pours contents in a cataract out on counter.*]

HAGAR

[*To negroes.*]

He'p yo'selves. [*Amazed, they do.*] An' now dat keg of bounce, how much dat?

DAVEY

[*His eyes popping.*]

De whole t'ing?

HAGAR

Shore, de whole t'ing.

DAVEY

I guess mus' be t'ree an' a half worth lef' in dat.

HAGAR

Yo' folks get to dat keg an' fill yo'selves up.   I allus been wantin' to gib yo' a party.   Dis my las' chance 'fore I go.

NEGROES

Yo' goin' away, Sistuh?   Where you goin'?
[*She does not answer. She looks on with detachment at the enthusiasm with which they accept her invitation.*]

EVA

You goin' back to Charleston an' lib wid yo' ma?

HAGAR

[*Seeming suddenly to realize that she has been spoken to.*]
Mebbe I is an' mebbe I goin' eben farder.

WILLIE MAY

Yo' goin' to Noo Yo'k wid yo' daughtuh?

DRAYTON

Mart'a here's goin' to Noo Yo'k. She gots a job.

HAGAR

Dat de trut'? Well, when you gets dere, say huddy to my gal fo' me.

DAVEY

You goin' be payin' fo' all dis, Sistuh?
    [HAGAR *takes roll of bills from bosom, separates one
    bill from the rest. Hands it to* DAVEY.]

HAGAR

Take um all out dis. [*Crosses to* VINA. *Drops on her
knees before her and with great tenderness opens the old
woman's hand and puts remaining bills in it, closes her fingers over them.*] Dis little good-bye present here from me
to you, Mauma. Don' yo' open um till I goes.

VINA

What yo' say, Daughtuh?

HAGAR

                    [*Louder.*]
Don' yo' open dis till I goes.

VINA

Yo' goin' away, Daughtuh?

HAGAR

Yes. I goin' away.

VINA

[*Anxiously.*]

Yo' ain' goin' far?

HAGAR

Not far from yo', Mauma. I got feelin' we goin' see each odder bery soon.

VINA

[*Distressed.*]

Promise me yo' ain't go far. I miss yo' too much. [HAGAR *nods assent.*] Won't be no singin' roun' here after yo' go—not like yo' sing. [*Brightening.*] Yo' 'member dat night 'fore yo' daughter gone off to be radio singer, how she an' we all sing togedder?

HAGAR

Fo' shore, I 'member. Ain't dat de las' time I see my gal?

VINA

[*Chuckling.*]

An' yo' gets me to sing de good-bye song for she?

HAGAR

[*Nodding.*]

Mauma, you sing good-bye to me. I'd like mighty well to hear yo' sing dat song when I goin'. Yo' do dat?

VINA

Yo' count on me, daughter. But yo' ain't goin' tonight? Ain't it powerful late?

HAGAR

[*Rising and starting back to counter.*]
Yes, I mus' be gettin' 'long.

VINA

Den I sing um now. [*Beginning to sing.*] "Oh, my daughter—"

HAGAR

[*Turning back and laying a restraining hand on her knee.*]
Not jus' yet, Mauma. I got my business to 'tend to 'fore I go. [*As she approaches counter,* DAVEY *proffers change.*] Don' gib me de change, son. Take um to de door an' t'row um far an' high. I t'rough wid money. I free now. [*Pause.*] Free as Gawd. [DAVEY *stares at her.*] Davey, I want yo' to do some writin' fo' me 'fore I goes. Get down dat paper an' pen yo' gots dere an' take down what I say. Come here, all yo' nigger. I wan' yo' to swear to dis writin'.

DAVEY

[*With pen and paper ready.*]
What yo' wants? Goin' write a letter?

HAGAR

I tell yo' what. Yo' jus' set um down.

DAVEY

What I say?

HAGAR

[Dictating.]

Dis night I—

DAVEY

Who's it to?

HAGAR

Jus' write um. *[Dictating.]* Dis night I strangle Gilly
Bluton to deat' wid my two han'. *[*DAVEY *starts to write,
then stops, transfixed. Severely.]* Yo' got dat? Write um,
I say.

> *[*DAVEY *writes. The negroes are spellbound. They
> stand speechless, motionless.* VINA *senses that some-
> thing is amiss.]*

VINA

What dat? What Hagar say?
> *[But no one even hears her.]*

HAGAR

[Dictating.]

I kill um 'cause all dese yeah he been my man an' he get
sick of me an' t'row me 'way. *[*DAVEY *stares at her like a
person hypnotized. Commandingly.]* Write um! *[Like a
person hypnotized,* DAVEY *writes. No one in the store
moves.]* You got dat? Read um!

DAVEY
[Reads.]
Dis night I strangle Gilly Bluton to deat' wid my two han'. I kill um 'cause all dese yeah he been my man—
[Bedlam breaks loose suddenly.]

NEGROES
'Tain't de trut'. Eberybody know it ain't de trut'. Gilly Bluton ain't neber been Hagar's man. Don' you write dat, Davey. T'row dat away. Mus' be you crazy, Sistuh.
[VINA is begging for enlightenment.]

EVA
[Running to VINA and yelling in her ear.]
Hagar say she been Gilly Bluton's woman. Dat ain't de trut', is it?
[VINA struggles to her feet.]

VINA
'Tain't de trut'. What you say dat for, Hagar? Ebery night you sleep in my cabin. You can't hab no man widout me knowin'.

HAGAR
[To DAVEY.]
Read um.

DAVEY
[Reads.]
I kill um 'cause all dese yeah he been my man an' he get sick of me an' t'row me 'way.
[HAGAR considers. Crowd is silent, fascinated.]

HAGAR
[*Dictating.*]
Dere ain't nobody dere but me.   Dere ain't nobody know
'bout um 'cept me.   [D<small>AVEY</small> *writes.*]   Now sign um, Hagar
Wentwuth.   [D<small>AVEY</small> *hesitates.*]   Sign um.
[D<small>AVEY</small> *signs.*]

NEGROES
[*Again simultaneously regaining their power of speech.*]
Don't you do um, Davey.   She ain't do um.   She crazy.
She ain't neber do um.   Ef she is do um it's good riddance.

VINA
Listen, everybody.   'Tain't de trut'.

HAGAR
[*Ignoring* V<small>INA</small>]
Now gimme de pen so as I can make de mark.   [*Reaches
over counter.   Takes pen from* D<small>AVEY</small>'s *lax hand.   Makes
her mark.   Folds paper.   Hands it to* D<small>AVEY</small>.]   I want you
fo' take um down to Sheriff Baggart in de mornin'.

NEGROES
No, don't you do it, Davey.   I ain't t'ink she done um at
all.   Hope she killed um daid a-plenty.

DRAYTON
Listen, everybody.   Hagar been right here all dis ebenin',
ain't she?   If anybody ax, dat's what we all goin' say.   We

all see Gilly Bluton 'live not more dan hour ago, an' eber
since then Hagar been right here.

NEGROES

Shore, she been right here. We all see um. We all goin'
swear she ain't leabe dis store.

HAGAR

Do lak I say, Davey. Take dat along to Proc Baggart in
de mawnin'.

DRAYTON

What yo' sen' dat fo', Hagar? Yo' can't get away. De
sheriff'll set his bloodhounds on yo'.

HAGAR

Dis is one nigger dose bloodhoun' of Proc Baggart's
ain't goin' to catch. [*Suddenly amused.*] Dat's shore goin'
to fidget um. Can't boast no more 'bout how he bloodhoun'
neber lose a nigger yet. Lis'en, eberybody. My ma say I
ain't no good less she wid me to tell me what to do. Well,
you go and tell um I do dis widout nobody tell me. I t'ink
um out all by myself. I t'ink um like dis. [*She leans on
counter and addresses them like a lawyer stating a case.*]
Fifteen year ago dat Gilly Bluton daid. Dey say at de
hospital five mo' minutes an' he ain't got a chance. Not a
Gawd's t'ing between dat yaller nigger an' he Gawd 'cept
only me. I gib um back he life. He life belong to me,
enty?

NEGROES

You shore sab' um. Dat's de Gawd's trut', Sistuh.

HAGAR

Well, I gone an' take back what belong to me. Dat's all—

VINA

What's Hagar sayin'? I can't hear um.
        [*Nobody pays her any attention.*]

HAGAR

—'cause after I save he life he take my— [*Catches her-self.*] —he try fo' t'row me 'way atter I used allus to be his 'oman. What de cops goin' to do wid dat? Dere ain't nobody dere 'cept me. Dere ain't nobody know about um 'cept me.

NEGROES

[*All together.*]

You're in your right, Sistuh. But de cops goin' get yo' jus' de same an' hang yo' in de 'lectric chair if yo' ain't get away from here mighty quick. What yo' want to sen' dat note for? Maybe they'd never know who done um.

HAGAR

I send um dat note 'cause cops got a way of axin' too much question. Dey ax yo' an' dey ax yo' till yo' is mos' crazy, an' yo' tells um more'n dey oughts to know. Well, now dey got um all set down in writin' who done um, an' why she done um, an' dey got no call to ax nobody nuttin'.

MINGO

Dey catch you though.   You best get goin' mighty quick.

HAGAR

[*Thoughtful.*]

Dat's de trut'.   Somebody might fin' Gilly Bluton by now and get the sheriff 'fore I makes my getaway.   I guess I better get goin'.

[VINA *can get nobody's attention.   With difficulty she again gets to her feet and hobbles back to counter.*]

VINA

What yo' sayin', daughter?   Nobody'll tell me what yo' sayin'.

HAGAR

I say I goin' now, Mauma.

VINA

Right now?

HAGAR

[*Nodding.*]

Right now.

VINA

Den now's de time fo' sing?

HAGAR

[*Nodding.*]

Now is de time fo' sing.

VINA

[Just in front of counter, turning to crowd.]
Hagar want us sing um good-bye. *[She is about to begin.
Then turns back anxiously to* HAGAR.*]* You goin' be seein'
me soon, daughter?
*[*HAGAR *gently leads the old woman back to her keg.]*

HAGAR
Bery soon, Mauma. *[Helps the old woman to sit. Kisses
her on forehead.]* Take care of yo'self, Mauma.

VINA
[To crowd.]
Let's we sing. *[Sings.]*
Sistuh Hagar, we goin' leabe yo' . . .
*[*HAGAR *returns slowly to counter.]*

WILLIE MAY
Yo' best not wait fo' no singin', Hagar.

HAGAR
[Nodding toward VINA.*]*
Lef' um sing. It make um feel better.

VINA
—We goin' to leabe yo' in de han',
Sistuh Hagar, we goin' to leabe yo' in de han' . . .
What's wrong with eberybody? Why nobody singin'?
[They turn toward VINA *and start to sing uncertainly.*

Quickly HAGAR *lifts the revolver from the counter and steps through the door onto the porch.* EVA *looks up and sees her go, carrying pistol.]*

EVA

[*Screaming.*]

Hagar, what yo' doin'!

[*All turn and some start forward. In the darkness beyond the door, there is a flash and loud report. The negroes huddle in door and windows, looking down at what lies below them on the porch floor.*]

A VOICE

Great God, she shoot herself.

ANOTHER VOICE

Gawd have mercy.

ANOTHER VOICE

Oh, my Jesus—

[*These ejaculations are followed by a profound silence in the group. They lean forward transfixed by what they see. Swaying obliviously back and forth on her keg, with her eyes turned away from the door, and her deaf old ears hearing only her own singing,* VINA's *quavering old voice sings on:*]

Oh, my daughter,
Goin' to leabe yo' in de han',

Goin' to leabe yo' in de han',
Oh, my daughter,
Goin' to leabe yo' in de han'
Ob de kin' Sab-yor.

CURTAIN